"You need a new heart but you are not waiting on a new heart to live. You are already living."

— Sashion Brown

"Your heart may be damaged but it is full of life and love."

— Amber RH

"You are a walking testament of who God is."

— Rayven Irons

"Your battles didn't break you. Neither will mine."

— Gabby Lamoore

"You've shown us that courage has meaning and that strength has value."

— Bernita

FUELED BY LOVE

FUELED BY LOVE

*The Power of Perspective
and the Way You See It Changes
Everything*

Cliff "The Gift" Wallace

Published by Fueled by Love Press
Houston, Texas

First Edition, 2026

ISBN: 979-8-9958653-0-8

Cover design by Justus Bailee | @justusbailee
Cover photography by Gerrick Walker | @gerrickwalkerimages

Medical Disclaimer: This book is a personal memoir and motivational work. It is not intended to provide medical advice, diagnosis, or treatment. The author's experiences with the LVAD, heart failure, and the transplant waitlist are shared for informational and inspirational purposes only. Always consult a qualified healthcare professional regarding any medical conditions or treatment decisions.

For my big brothers Nick and Jule.

This one is for you. Always.

"If you really got a pure heart, you're gonna win in the end. Remember that."

— Cliff "The Gift" Wallace

Contents

The experiences and conversations in this book have been reconstructed from memory. Some details may have been compressed or adjusted for narrative clarity. The author has made every effort to tell his story truthfully and accurately.

For permissions, speaking inquiries, or bulk orders contact: clifton.wallace@gmail.com

Follow the journey: @iamcliffthegift

Fueled by Love.

Acknowledgements

To my mom. You are my rock and at 42 years old I still wake up wanting to make you proud. That never changed. That will never change. Everything I build has your name on it even when I don't say it out loud.

To my dad, Big Cliff. I've been Lil Cliff since the day I was born and I wouldn't have it any other way. I see you in the way I move, the way I carry myself, the way I show up. I got a lot of you in me and I'm proud of that.

To Mike. You're more than my little brother. You're my best friend. We don't always see eye to eye and we don't always move the same way but at our core we are one and the same. And if I know anything about this life I know we will always show up for each other. Always.

To Nick. I miss you bro. I wish we had more time. This book started with you. You planted something in me long before I was ready to grow it and now here it is. Full circle. This one's yours too.

To Jule. I miss you bro. I never got to tell you to your face how proud I was of the man you became. To know where you came from and to see where you were when you left us, I find peace in knowing you were finally finding yours. I carry that.

To Maliyah. Shrimp, I love you kid. I made a promise to your Nanny Lula that I would always be there for you and I mean to keep it no matter where life takes us. You will always be my daughter at heart and I will always answer when you call. Until my last breath.

To this community. You really don't understand what you've done for me. Half the time I don't fully understand it either. But you give me purpose. You give me reason to keep going even on the days when keeping going is the scariest thing I've ever done. I appreciate you more than I'll ever be able to say properly.

And to God. Thank you. I mean that with everything in me. Thank you for the good in my life and thank you for what some people would call the bad. I am grateful for all of it. Because when I look back honestly there has been so much goodness in everything, even the hard things, even the painful things, even the things I wouldn't have chosen. It was all working on me. It was all working for me.

Thank you.

Fueled by Love.

Cliff "The Gift" Wallace

Foreword

A Note From Those Who Were Here

These words were not solicited by a publisher. They were not written by critics or colleagues or anyone with a credential that qualifies them to speak on literature. They were written by people who came to know a man across social media, on Facebook, Instagram, and TikTok, in the middle of something that should have broken him and could not look away. People drawn in not by a highlight reel or some bullshit facade but by something rarer. Honesty. Vulnerability. A man who showed up as himself every single day regardless of what that day cost him. No filter. No performance. Just some real shit, and sometimes that shit was ugly and hard and cost him more than most people will ever know. And they stayed rockin' anyway. People who were sitting in hospital waiting rooms for sick brothers. People fighting cancer, MS, fibromyalgia, strokes, autoimmune disease, heart failure. People who were at their lowest point and found their way to his corner of the internet and decided to stay. That is the power of authenticity. This shit is what real community looks like. That's fellowship in its truest form. And real talk? It still blows my mind every damn day. These are their words. Unedited. Unscripted. Freely given.

"Your battles didn't break you. Neither will mine."
— Gabby Lamoore

"I started following you at my weakest point. I saw your journey and it encouraged me to keep my head up, stay faithful, rely on God, and advocate for myself. I received my transplant organ December 16th, 2025, and I know yours is coming. God makes no mistakes."
— Chalita Dudley

"Your story has taught me that even in the darkest and weakest moments of life it's still possible to love wholeheartedly, to give freely, to hope deeply."
— Sashion Brown

"You need a new heart but you are not waiting on a new heart to live. You are already living."
— TJ Williams

"Your strength has gotten me through my worst moment. Through your videos, you never complain, even on days when you could have."
— Tamika Denise Townsend

"I began this journey with you just browsing Facebook one day two and a half years ago, sitting in the waiting room at a heart appointment for my brother. Right from the first post I saw you, I followed you right then."
— Debra Jackson-Noble Williams

"Following your journey has encouraged and inspired me to come to terms with my own health challenge and MS diagnosis. The way you show up and move through life's challenges gives others going through difficult moments hope."
— Rayven Irons

"You are a walking testament of who God is."
— Thelma L. Taylor

"Your story is to help someone else. You were chosen for such a time as this. Good, bad, ugly days, but you're STILL. HERE."
— Maria D'Aguilar Allie

"Watching your videos has taught me to be more transparent about my illness. I have had an autoimmune disease since I was 16. I wouldn't talk about it or show my battle scars. You taught me it was okay."
— Bernita

"You've shown us that courage has meaning and that strength has value."
— Amber RH

"Your heart may be damaged but it is full of life and love."
— Tina Debonnett

"Your strength through this journey is truly inspiring. Your impact reaches far beyond what you may realize."
— Monet Franklin, Dallas, Texas

"Always remember where you are right now in your life is what you prayed and cried for not too long ago. Always be grateful."
— Maria McLean

"You've truly inspired me to stop procrastinating and start living life to its fullest. Your story gave me the push I needed."
— Krystal Cartharn

My God! I've had the privilege of knowing Cliff far beyond the pages of this book. He's been by my side through some of the most difficult moments in my life—times that came with real weight, real uncertainty, and more than a few tears.

That's why Fueled by Love feels so real to me. This isn't theory—it's lived. I've seen Cliff embody the very principles he writes about— showing up when it felt like it wouldn't matter, choosing discipline when circumstances didn't line up, and continuing to move forward when you've been dealt a bad hand.

At its heart, this piece is a reminder that we don't need perfect conditions to take the next step. With cues like showing up anyway, controlling what you can, stacking small wins, eliminating excuses, and protecting your mind, Cliff lays out a simple, honest way to navigate life when shit hits the fan.

There are lessons in these pages that stay with you—the kind that meet you right where you are and push you forward. Not by waiting for things to get easier, but by becoming stronger within it.

To say I'm proud of Cliff would be an understatement—not just for writing this book, but for living it. It's up from here baby.

Don't take this book for granted.

My boy put his heart into this.

— Justus Bailee

I love this. I loved watching your journey. It taught me that you should never give up and don't ever listen to what people tell you. Watching you continue to be yourself despite being on the transplant list and hoping that one day you will get a heart. You continue to stay strong and positive. You continue to be a positive influence on the community, and I know that the kids in the schools love it when Uncle Cliff and Santa Cliff come around to make their day. You inspired me to get more involved in my community by giving back. I will continue to donate to your projects as long as you're taking donations.

And how you always used to end your greetings in the morning back in the day—

"And if you haven't heard it yet, just know that you are loved and I love you. And when I say that, I mean that, so believe that. So go out there and have an amazing day."
— @drbreknows

Imma be honest lovely. I don't know how to respond. Watching you navigate has been a blessing and it's amazing to see you handle it with such grace. It hasn't reminded me about my own life or taught me anything in particular as the things you stand for and tools you use we are aligned with. It is, however, a gentle reminder that we are stronger than we believe ourselves to be. And that life is really about the mindset.

— Adriyan Rae

No matter how weak you feel in the moment. Never lose your faith in God.

Seeing how you were healthy and doing great then everything started to change, and you didn't let it affect you. You got up and proceeded to get stronger than you were before. Mentally and physically, it made me feel like I can handle all the bad things in life. Knowing that someday it will be okay.

Seeing how you carry yourself even with an end-stage heart disease, made me look up to you and how I should carry myself and not let the bad things affect what really matters. What matters is the present moment.

It taught me to not take things for granted because anything can happen.

You taught me to still find happiness even in the bad times.

— Maliyah (Shrimpy)

I've had the privilege of knowing Cliff for several years, and what stands out most is not just his strength, but the grace with which he carries it. Despite living with a serious heart condition, he chooses joy, purpose, and service — pouring into his community, uplifting children, and giving generously year after year. You would never know the weight he carries unless he told you, and that quiet resilience is what makes his story so powerful. This book offers a glimpse into the heart of a man who refuses to give up, and instead chooses to live fully, love deeply, and inspire others to do the same. I invite you to turn these pages and experience his journey for yourself.

— Hannah Young

This is who was watching, praying, holding on alongside him, being fueled by the same love that fueled the man who wrote what follows.

If their words found you before his did, you are exactly where you are supposed to be.

Turn the page.

We are hard pressed on every side, but not crushed. Perplexed, but not in despair. Persecuted, but not abandoned. Struck down, but not destroyed.

— 2 Corinthians 4:8-9

Introduction

This shit ain't about surviving. This book is about living while the surviving is still happening.

I'm not here to sugarcoat shit and say it all gets better. This ain't that and I ain't them. I'm here to tell you that you can be better right now, in the middle of it, before it gets anywhere.

This book was not written for the person who made it through. It was written for the person still in it.

I don't have a PhD, I'm not a therapist, and I'm damn sure not a doctor. I don't have a happily ever after to sell you because I'm still mid-story. What I have is a life that has put me through the absolute ringer in ways I wouldn't wish on anyone, and a set of truths that have kept me standing through all of it. That's the only credential that matters here.

I wanted something written from inside the fire, not after the fact. I needed words that didn't make me wait until I was healed to finally have something useful to say. When I couldn't find it I understood that meant I was supposed to write it. So I did. From inside it. In real time. With everything still unresolved.

This is for the person carrying something right now that most people around them will never see. If you've been waiting for permission to just feel your shit, or you're tired of being told to stay positive by people who aren't carrying what you're carrying, this is for you. I see you. I am you.

What you're about to read is not a formula. It's a perspective. Fourteen chapters built around the shifts that have kept me moving through a total shitstorm. These aren't theories I thought up over coffee. This is lived. Every word here was pressure tested by a life that tried to break me.

You don't have to be going through what I'm going through to need what's in these pages. You just have to be human. And you just have to be willing to see things differently.

That's it. That's all this asks.

Fueled by Love. 🖤
Cliff

Photo by Gerrick Walker | @gerrickwalkerimages

Prologue

The Man in the Storm

You may not control all the events that happen to you, but you can decide not to be reduced by them.

— Maya Angelou

Nobody gets out of this life without going through something.

Not the ones who look like they have it all together. Not the ones who smile through everything like none of it costs them anything. Every single person

The question has never been whether the storm comes. The question is who you decide to be while you're standing in it.

I'm writing this from inside mine, not from a comfortable place on the other side looking back with the luxury of hindsight. Not from a season of restoration where everything worked out and I finally have the distance to reflect.

I'm writing this right now, in the middle of it, with the weight of uncertainty on my chest and the kind of faith that doesn't come from having answers but from deciding to believe anyway.

There is a machine keeping my heart pumping as these words are being written. A device called an LVAD, a left ventricular assist device, that does the work my heart can no longer fully do on its own.

I carry it in a pack around my waist every single day. I sleep with it. I shower around it. I work out with this shit. I build with it. I live with it. That shit is my life right now and I wouldn't trade what it's taught me for anything. And I'm on a waiting list for a heart transplant that hasn't come yet.

The device is a Medtronic HVAD. It was implanted on March 10th, 2021. Eighty-five days later, on June 3rd, 2021, Medtronic stopped all distribution and sale of the system. Physicians were notified to cease new implants immediately. It was discontinued. Pulled from the market. And it's still in my chest.

I made a decision a long time ago not to live inside that fear. But I'd be lying if I said the thought never visits.

It visits. I just don't let it stay.

I'm telling you because you need to know who is talking to you in this book. You need to know that what's written here wasn't figured out in a comfortable room somewhere. It was forged inside real uncertainty. Real loss. Real weight.

And I'm writing it because someone needs it right now, not eventually.

Maybe that's you.

Maybe you picked this book up because something in your life is not going the way you planned. Maybe you've been hit with news you didn't see coming. Maybe you've lost someone who was supposed to still be here. Maybe the relationship you built your world around is gone. Maybe your body is failing you. Maybe your finances are pressing on you from every direction.

Maybe you look at your life and you genuinely cannot find the light in it right now. I understand that feeling more than you know.

I've lost two brothers. Nick and Jule. Both gone too fucking soon. Both men who shaped who I am in ways I'm still discovering. Grief like that doesn't leave. It just changes shape over time. Some days it's a dull ache in the background. Other days it walks right into the room and sits down next to you like it never left.

I know what it is to carry something heavy and still be expected to function like it's not there.

The darkness is real. The pain is real. Don't let anyone tell you otherwise.

None of that means the goodness isn't also real. Both things exist at the same time, and your life is shaped less by which one is present and more by which one you train yourself to see.

That's the whole book in one sentence, and I want to be clear about what it isn't. It isn't pretending, and it isn't the kind of toxic positivity I have no patience for and I don't think you do either.

This is about the lens you look through and how that lens, more than your circumstances, more than your resources, more than your past, determines what your life produces in you and what you produce in it.

I believe that with everything in me. Not because someone taught it to me in a classroom, but because I've lived it.

I've been in rooms where I had every reason to give up and found a reason to keep going instead. I've lost people I loved deeply and discovered that love doesn't actually leave when people do. I've had my body fail me in ways that should have broken my spirit and found out my spirit was built for more than I knew.

There's a man in the Bible named Job who I keep coming back to. Job lost everything, and not gradually. All of it came at once, his children, his health, his wealth, everything that made his life look like a life worth living stripped away in what felt like a single breath.

And the people closest to him, the ones who were supposed to show up, mostly showed up to question him. To suggest he must have done something to deserve it. To offer explanations that made them feel better about his suffering without actually helping him carry it.

Job didn't have answers. He had questions. Real ones. Loud ones. The kind you only ask when the pain is so heavy you stop worrying about how the question sounds.

But here's the thing about Job that never leaves me. He held on anyway.

Not because he understood what was happening. Not because someone explained it in a way that made it make sense. He held on because somewhere underneath all the loss and all the confusion and all the unanswered questions there was something in him that refused to let the darkness write the final word about his life.

This book is my testimony. Built from the inside of the storm. Written for the person who needs to know that what they're going through is not the whole story.

The goodness is still there even when you can't see it yet. Love, real love that fuels you when nothing else can, is enough to carry you through anything life puts in front of you.

You don't have to have it figured out to keep going. You just have to be willing to see it differently.

That's where we start. Right here. In the middle of it. And it starts with how you see where you are.

Chapter 1 — It Starts With How You See It

Life is 10% what happens to you and 90% how you react to it.

— Charles R. Swindoll

Two people can go through the same experience and come out completely different people.

They may experience the same diagnosis, same loss, same heartbreak, same financial collapse, same betrayal, same storm. Everything about the external situation identical. Same starting point. Same weight. Same wreckage left behind when it was over.

One person comes out bitter, closed, smaller than they were before. Hardened in a way that makes them difficult to reach and difficult to love. They carry the experience like a wound that never healed because somewhere along the way they decided the wound was the story.

The other comes out deeper, sharper, more intentional, more alive in ways they weren't before the hard thing happened. They carry the experience too, but they carry it differently. Like something that shaped them instead of something that broke them.

The same storm, two completely different people on the other side of it, and the difference was never the storm. It was the lens.

Most of us spend our energy trying to change our circumstances when the real work, the work that actually changes a life, happens at the level of perception. It happens at the level of how we interpret what's happening to us and what meaning we decide to give it. We exhaust ourselves trying to fix the external situation when the internal one is what's actually running the show.

Real things happen. Real pain lands and leaves marks that don't fully disappear.

But here's what changed everything for me. The clarity didn't come after the circumstances changed. The clarity is what changed the circumstances. It changed what they meant and therefore what they produced in me and what I did with them. I didn't wait until life got easier to start seeing differently. Seeing differently is what eventually made life easier.

Two people, same storm, different lenses, different lives. I've watched this play out more times than I can count. I've watched people go through things that would break most people and somehow come out with a depth and a warmth and a wisdom that people who've never been tested simply don't have. There's something in those people that you can feel when you're around them. A groundedness. A realness. Like they've been somewhere and came back with something the rest of us are still looking for.

I've also watched people go through far less and never recover. Not because they were weaker. Not because they deserved it. But because somewhere in the experience they decided what it meant. They labeled it, sealed it, and lived inside that label for the rest of their life. The story they told themselves about what happened became the walls they lived inside.

The label you put on your experience becomes the life you live.

Real perspective is harder than denial. Denial lets you look away. Real perspective requires you to look directly at the hard thing, see it clearly, feel it fully, and then make a conscious decision about what meaning you're going to build from it. Not what meaning it automatically carries, but what meaning you choose to give it, and that distinction, what you choose versus what automatically arrives, is the whole game.

I was 26. Working hard, in the gym lifting heavy, out in the clubs making myself available because your boy been fine in the most humble way. Up late, dry scooping pre workout with no chaser like it was crack in the 90s because sleep felt optional when life felt this good. My diet was whatever I wanted it to be because I figured the gym canceled it out. 26 year old logic. I do not recommend it. I had money in my pocket and the kind of confidence that comes from looking good on the outside while paying zero attention to what was happening on the inside. I was young and I was moving like I was invincible because nothing had told me otherwise yet.

Then my heart did.

The diagnosis came at 26 and landed in a way I wasn't prepared for. Not because I fell apart. I didn't. I was still too young and too confident for it to fully break through. But it cracked something open. A small window that let a little bit of reality in even though I wasn't ready to climb through it yet. It woke me up just enough to know what was real without waking me up enough to actually change how I was moving.

So I kept going. Filed it in the back of my mind. Told myself I'd deal with it, manage it, handle it the way I handled everything else. And for a while that worked, or at least it felt like it did. Because the most dangerous lens you can look through isn't the one built from bitterness or grief. It's the one built from comfort and confidence. The one that says I'm fine, I'm strong, I've got time, this applies to other people not to me.

That lens is quiet. It doesn't announce itself. It just sits there behind everything you do, shaping every decision, every habit, every thing you tell yourself you'll get around to eventually. And it keeps working on you until reality finally shows up and takes it off your face whether you're ready or not.

I didn't always see clearly, and there was a long season in my life where I looked at everything happening around me and the only story I could find was loss. What I couldn't do anymore. What had been taken. The gap between where I was and where I thought I should be by now. I was measuring my life against a version of it that wasn't coming, and every day that version didn't show up felt like another confirmation that something was fundamentally wrong.

That lens made everything heavy. When everything feels heavy you stop moving the way you're supposed to move. You start making smaller, safer decisions because the bigger ones feel too risky when you're already carrying so much. You start shrinking into the size of your fear instead of expanding into the size of your potential. And the worst part is you don't even realize it's happening. You just slowly become a smaller version of yourself and call it being realistic.

I know what that feels like from the inside. I also know the moment it started to shift.

It wasn't dramatic. It wasn't a lightning bolt or a vision or a single conversation that changed everything overnight. Real change rarely works that way regardless of what the highlight reels tell you. It was a slow realization, arriving in pieces over time, that the way I was seeing my life was costing me more than the circumstances themselves. The story I was telling myself about what was happening was doing more damage than what was actually happening.

And once I saw that I couldn't unsee it, and I didn't want to.

If the lens was the problem, the lens was also the solution. And the lens was mine. Nobody had given it to me and nobody could take it from me. I had more power over my own life than I had been giving myself credit for, and that realization, as uncomfortable as it was to sit with, was also one of the most freeing things I'd ever felt.

Moving the right direction slowly still gets you somewhere worth being, and moving the wrong direction fast just gets you further from where you actually need to be.

Nothing that happens to you comes with a fixed meaning. Every experience, every loss, every diagnosis, every betrayal, every setback, every detour comes to you as raw material. What you build from that material is determined by the questions you ask, the stories you tell, and the lens you choose to look through. The raw material doesn't change. But what you make of it is entirely up to you.

You do not always get to choose what happens. But you always get to choose the meaning you build from it, and that is not a small power, that is the most significant power you carry, and no circumstance, no person, no season of loss can take it from you unless you hand it over.

The storm is real. Feel it. Survive it. But refuse to let it write the final story about who you are and what your life means. That story belongs to you. It has always belonged to you. No circumstance, no person, no season of loss has the authority to write it for you unless you hand them the pen.

Don't hand them the pen. It starts with how you see it. But seeing it clearly requires you to first stop arguing with it.

Chapter 2 — Accept What Is, Then Move

A man is given two lives. The second begins when he realizes he only has one.

Most of us spend years arguing with reality.

Internally, silently, in the way we resist what's already true. In the way we replay what should have happened instead of dealing with what did. In the way we stay frozen between the life we planned and the life we're actually living, unable to fully commit to either one because committing to the real one means letting go of the imagined one. That argument may cost us everything.

It's not because the pain isn't real. It is. But here's what nobody tells you about fighting reality. Reality always wins.

Reality doesn't move because you refuse to accept it. Grief doesn't leave on your schedule no matter how hard you push back against it.

The moment you stop wasting strength fighting what is already true is the moment you finally have strength to do something about it.

The first time my body introduced me to its limits I was 26. I would spend the next decade living like that introduction was a one time meeting, a warning I had acknowledged and moved past rather than something I was still carrying. I told myself I had handled it. Filed it away. Built a life around the story that the hard chapter was behind me.

I was in LA. I had built something that felt like the life I was supposed to have. A community around me. A city that matched my energy. Everything moving the way it was supposed to. Somewhere in the back of my mind the health situation existed, but it wasn't the main character of my story anymore. I had outrun it, or so I told myself.

Life has a way of correcting those stories. I came back to Houston. At 37 it introduced itself again, and it did so properly this time. This introduction left no room for the story I'd been telling myself about having outrun anything. This time it wasn't a warning. It was a reckoning.

It was during the pandemic. The world had already shut down. Hospitals were operating differently, overwhelmed and restructured in ways nobody had ever seen before. When I came in they didn't have a room for me right away. So for about eleven hours I was in the hallway, a hospital bed in a corridor with blood work being drawn and tests being run and monitors attached, people moving past me with their own emergencies while I lay there waiting on results that were going to tell me something I wasn't sure I was ready to hear. That was a long ass eleven hours man. Like long as hell.

Those eleven hours in that hallway were some of the longest of my life. My mind wouldn't slow down. It was running through everything, not just what was happening in that moment but my entire life, childhood, teenage years, the man I had become, and then the future, the version of my life I had always believed was still ahead of me. The wife I hadn't met yet. The children I hadn't had. The goals and dreams I had carried for years that felt suddenly and terrifyingly fragile in a way they never had before.

That was the fear that sat with me in that hallway. Not just the fear of what was happening to my body. The fear of an unlived life. The fear that the future I had always assumed was coming might not come. That the version of myself I had always believed in, the husband, the father, the man who got to see his dreams become real, might never get the chance to exist.

Maybe you've sat somewhere waiting on news and felt that same thing. Not just fear of the outcome but fear of everything you haven't done yet. Fear of the version of yourself that might not get its chance. That fear has a specific weight to it. I know you know what I mean.

That's a specific kind of terror that doesn't have a clean name. Let that land for a second.

After eleven hours the results came back and they moved me to the ICU. And that night, the night before they were going to put a balloon pump in me to help my heart function while they figured out what came next, a doctor came and sat with me.

She explained everything. The severity of what was happening. What the numbers meant. What the procedure involved. What was at stake. She was honest with me in a way that took courage on her part, the kind of honesty that medical professionals sometimes hold back because they're trying to protect you from the full weight of what they know.

She didn't hold back. And somewhere in that conversation we both cried.

She didn't talk to me like a doctor that night. She talked to me like a mother talking to her child. Like a big sister who needed her little brother to hear something true. And when everything had been said that needed to be said I looked at her and told her I was going to be just fine. I meant it. She needed me to mean it. And somewhere between the tears and the machines and everything still uncertain I think we both believed it.

I want you to sit with that image for a moment because it says everything that words alone can't fully carry. A doctor, trained to deliver difficult news with clinical composure, sitting in an ICU room during a pandemic, crying with her patient the night before a major procedure.

No more buffer. No more filing it away. No more telling myself I had outrun something or that it was manageable or that I had time to deal with it later. The woman with the medical degree and the years of training was sitting across from me with tears in her eyes and there was simply no version of denial left available to me.

I didn't fall apart. That's not who I am. But I felt it. Fully. For the first time in a long time I let the weight of what was actually happening land on me without trying to deflect it or manage it or perform strength around it. It was just me and the truth of my situation sitting in the same room together with nowhere to go and no reason to pretend otherwise.

And that was the beginning of something I didn't expect. I had spent a long time being the person who didn't allow himself to feel, who understood strength as the absence of emotion, who believed that keeping it together meant keeping everything inside. That's what I had been taught. What most men are taught. That tears are weakness. That vulnerability is exposure. That a man handles things quietly and moves on without making it anyone else's burden.

But alone in that ICU room with a doctor who was willing to be human with me, I started to understand something that has continued to shape how I move through the world ever since.

Feeling is not weakness. Feeling is humanity. Feeling is the ability to sit with fear and uncertainty and grief and let it move through you instead of building walls to keep it out. The men who never learn that spend their whole lives carrying weight that was never meant to be carried alone in silence, and it shows up eventually whether they invite it or not.

Acceptance is not agreement. It's just honesty about your starting point.

Acceptance is the honest acknowledgment that this is where you are.

It's not where you planned to be. It's not where you deserve to be. It's just where you are right now. And that honest acknowledgment is one of the most powerful things a person can do, because it redirects all the energy you were using to fight the present toward actually building the future. You cannot build forward while your energy is pointed backward at something that has already decided to be true.

Acceptance is just being honest about your starting point. And from an honest starting point you can actually move.

That quote has stayed with me in a place that doesn't have a name. There was a version of my life I was living before that ICU room, before that conversation, before those eleven hours in a hallway watching my future flash in front of me. A version where I moved through the world like there was always more time. Like the shot clock wasn't running. Like the things that mattered could wait because there was always tomorrow.

That version ended in an ICU room during a pandemic, and a new one began.

I think about the man I was in LA, convinced the hard chapter was behind him, and I think about the man I became sitting in that Houston hospital facing something that made every previous version of hard look different in hindsight. Those two men had the same name and the same face, but they had a completely different relationship with reality. The LA version was living with one eye closed, choosing not to look at what was still present because looking felt like inviting it back in. The Houston version had both eyes open. Reality didn't give him the option of one eye closed anymore.

Both eyes open, as uncomfortable as it is, is the only way to actually see your life clearly enough to build something real inside it.

Everything changed after that, quietly, the way real change actually happens. I started smiling more, not performing happiness but actually feeling it. I started expressing more, letting things land instead of deflecting them. Living in a way that matched the value I now understood time actually had.

We are all on borrowed time with a shot clock we cannot see ticking down. No exceptions. The only difference between me and someone who hasn't had a moment that forced them to face that truth is that I can no longer pretend otherwise. My reality made denial impossible. And as painful as that was, it gave me something most people spend their whole lives waiting for.

It gave me my second life, and yours begins the moment you stop arguing with your first one.

You don't need your world to fall apart before you can be honest about where you are.

Now what is a question that moves. It points forward. That's the whole difference. Instead of spinning in how you got here, you're already asking what comes next.

That's acceptance. Not a feeling. A decision. A daily, sometimes hourly, decision to stop fighting what is and start building what's next.

The dark moments are real. Feel them. Honor them. Don't rush past them like they don't deserve your attention because they do. Grief is real. Fear is real. The uncertainty of not knowing how things are going to unfold is absolutely real. Sit with it long enough to actually feel it.

Just don't get stuck there.

The light is real. The second life is real. And the morning waiting on the other side of it is real too. None of it shows up while you're still standing in the dark arguing with it.

Accept what is. Then move. Your second life is waiting. The hardest part of moving isn't the circumstances. It's the voice inside you that keeps telling you not to.

Chapter 3 — Your Mind Can Be Your Cage or Your Freedom

Whether you think you can or you think you can't, you're right.

— Henry Ford

There is a voice in your head right now.

Not a metaphor. An actual voice that narrates your life, interprets your experiences, tells you what things mean, and decides before you've even fully processed a situation whether you're going to be okay or not. That voice is running constantly, in the background of every decision you make, every risk you consider, every dream you almost chase before it talks you out of it.

Most people never stop to question that voice. They treat it like truth. Like because it's coming from inside their own head it must be accurate, must be reflecting reality back to them clearly. So they listen. They obey. They let it set the ceiling on their life without ever asking whether the ceiling is real or just a story the voice keeps repeating.

Here's what most people don't tell you about that voice though. It doesn't always hold you back with doubt. Sometimes it holds you back with confidence. Sometimes the most paralyzing thing the voice can say isn't you can't do this. Sometimes it's you don't have to rush. It's coming. You're built for it. When the time is right it's going to happen.

That version of the voice is the most dangerous one because it doesn't feel like fear. It feels like faith.

I know that voice personally. For most of my adult life mine didn't whisper that I wasn't capable. It whispered that I didn't need to move yet. That everything I was supposed to have and become was already written. That the timing would align when it was supposed to align. That I was Cliff The Gift and gifts don't have to chase anything. The gift gets recognized. The gift arrives when it's supposed to arrive.

So I waited.

I was always moving, always building something. But underneath all of it was this deep seated belief that the big things, the real things, were going to happen on their own timeline and there was no need to push. The book I kept meaning to write. The acting I pursued in LA and then let drift when life got complicated. Content creation I fell into but never fully committed to the way I knew I should. The ideas and ventures I kept sketching out in my head but never fully launched because the timing never felt right.

All of it sitting in a waiting room inside me while I told myself the timing wasn't right yet.

The book alone. I should have written this years ago. The ideas were there. My story was there. The need to say something was there. But the voice kept telling me there would be a better time. When things settled down. When the health situation resolved. When everything was aligned just right and the conditions were finally perfect for me to do what I was already built to do.

Then last year as summer was ending I finally stopped listening to it. I opened up and started. Actually started. Not planning it, not thinking about it, not telling myself it was coming. Writing it. Moving on it. It felt like something breaking open that had been sealed for too long.

A week later I was back in the hospital. A scare with my LVAD site, a possible infection, the kind of thing that when you're living with a device keeping your heart running you don't take lightly. A week in that bed. And just like that the book went back on the shelf. Back to the waiting room. Back to later.

I'm finishing it now, from inside the same uncertainty that interrupted it. Because I finally understood something I should have understood years ago.

The conditions were never going to be perfect. They aren't perfect now. The version of readiness I was waiting for doesn't exist. And every year I spent waiting was a year the book didn't exist, the fully committed version of me didn't exist.

That's what the voice cost me. Time. That's what it cost me.

The voice in your head is not always telling you the truth. Sometimes it's telling you the most comfortable lie it can find. The comfortable lie isn't always I can't do this. Sometimes it's I'll get to it when the time is right. And because it doesn't feel like fear, you follow it faithfully.

Real patience and counterfeit patience look almost identical from the outside. The difference is what's happening underneath. Real patience is trusting the process while you're actively working within it. Moving every day toward something even when the results aren't visible yet. Doing the thing before the conditions are perfect because you understand that the doing is what creates the conditions.

Counterfeit patience sounds like wisdom, feels like peace, and is actually just fear or comfort dressed up in spiritual language. And because it doesn't feel like fear, you follow it faithfully. Convincingly, even to yourself.

One day you look up and the waiting has become your life. Denzel Washington gave a commencement speech that has never left me. He asked the graduating class to imagine being on their deathbed at the end of their life. Standing around that bed are the ghosts. Ghosts of everything they never did. The ideas they never acted on. The gifts they never fully used. The dreams they kept postponing for a better time that never came.

Those ghosts aren't peaceful. They're angry. They came to you specifically because you had the ability to bring them to life. You didn't. Now they have to be buried with you.

I felt that deeply the first time I heard it, not as a cautionary tale about someone else but as a mirror. I've met some of my own ghosts already. The things I put off. The moves

I delayed. The version of myself I kept promising to become when the time was right. An acting career I started in LA and let drift. The book you're holding that should have existed sooner. The content platform I built halfway and then managed instead of maximized because the voice kept telling me I had time to take it seriously later.

I'm still here, which means I still have a chance to bring some of them to life, but the clock is running. I know that now in a way I can't unfeel. The LVAD on my hip is a daily reminder that time is not a resource I have an unlimited supply of. None of us do. Most people just don't have something that reminds them of it every single day.

Your thoughts become beliefs when you repeat them enough. Those beliefs quietly become your identity. And your identity determines the size of the life you're willing to step into.

The voice in your head becomes the atmosphere you live in.

You can change the atmosphere. That's what Ford was really saying. Whether you think you can or you think you can't, you're right, not because thinking makes it so, but because what you believe about yourself determines what you'll attempt, and what you attempt determines what becomes possible. The voice sets the ceiling. You get to decide how high that ceiling goes. The practice of questioning that voice, refusing to let it be the final word, choosing a different story even when the old one feels more familiar, that practice changes things over time. The voice doesn't disappear. You just stop giving it the authority to decide.

Whose voice are you listening to right now, in the quiet moments when nobody's watching and you're deciding whether to move or stay still? Is it building you or containing you? Is it pushing you forward or giving you beautifully reasonable explanations for why now isn't the right time?

The mind that keeps you safe can also keep you small. The voice that sounds like confidence can be doing the same damage as the voice that sounds like fear. At some point you have to decide which one you actually need more.

Here's the thing I had to come to terms with about myself. And it connects directly back to that voice.

I spent years searching for my purpose. Not passively. Actively. Trying things. Pursuing directions. Pulling myself in multiple directions because I have real strengths and real interests and genuine passion in more than one area. And that breadth, which should have been an asset, became part of the problem. Because I kept letting myself get pulled. Content here. Fitness there. Acting. The book. All of it real, all of it mine, but spread so damn thin that nothing ever got the full version of me it deserved.

I kept blurring the line between patience and procrastination. Between confidence and counterfeit confidence. And then I'd look up and realize I was standing in the same spot I'd been in a year before. I was moving but never in one direction long enough to arrive anywhere.

What the LVAD and the transplant list and everything that came with it forced me to do was stop. Not by choice. By necessity. And in the stopping I saw something I had been too busy to see while I was running.

I had been walking in my purpose the whole time. I just kept rejecting it. Second guessing it. Spreading myself across everything instead of going all in on the thing I was actually built for.

The crazy shit, as painful and uncertain and unfinished as it still is, did what years of searching couldn't. It made me stop running from myself long enough to finally see who I actually am and what I'm actually here to do.

Maybe that's what your searching has been doing for you too. Not keeping you from your purpose. Walking you toward it whether you recognized it or not.

The cage was never locked. You just kept listening to the voice that told you not to open it. Stop listening. Open it. Once you open that cage you're going to find out that some of what's waiting on the other side of it isn't comfortable, and that discomfort isn't a sign something is wrong, it's actually the whole point of opening it.

Chapter 4 — Pain Is Not the Enemy

The wound is the place where the light enters you.

— Rumi

Nobody chooses pain.

Nobody volunteers for the diagnosis, the loss, the betrayal, the season that strips everything familiar away and leaves you standing in the middle of your own life wondering how you got here and how you get out.

Pain arrives uninvited. Always. It doesn't knock or ask permission or check your schedule. It just shows up.

The first response is to fight it, to resist it, to look for the fastest way through it or around it or out of it. But what if the fastest way out is actually through it? What if the thing you've been trying to escape is also the thing trying to change you? What if pain is not the enemy?

It can sound dismissive. Like I'm minimizing real suffering with a reframe that looks good on paper but falls apart the moment you're actually inside something breaking you. That's not what I'm saying.

I'm not asking you to pretend pain doesn't hurt. It does. Deeply. In ways that change you at a cellular level and leave marks that don't fully disappear. I'm not asking you to skip the grief or rush the healing or perform gratitude for things that deserve your full honest emotional attention.

What I'm asking you to consider is whether pain, alongside everything it takes, also has something to give.

I've lived on both sides of that question. I've been in the middle of something taking from me in every direction and found something being deposited at the same time that I couldn't have received any other way, and I'm not offering you theory when I say that, I'm offering you testimony from someone who has lived it.

Comfort is a terrible teacher. It keeps you exactly where you are. It has no reason to push you deeper, make you stronger, force you to find reserves you didn't know existed, or strip away the things that were never serving you in the first place. Comfort is warm and familiar and it will keep you exactly the size you are indefinitely.

The version of yourself you're most proud of, the depth you carry, the wisdom you've accumulated, the specific quality of presence you bring to hard situations, where did that come from? Not from the easy seasons. From the ones that required something from you that you weren't sure you had.

Pain is where that gets built, not because suffering is noble or because hard times are something to seek out, but because the human capacity for real lasting change is almost always activated by difficulty rather than comfort.

Pressure produces things that ease simply cannot.

I believe this life was designed for me to live exactly the way I have lived it. The diagnosis at 26. The years of moving like I was untouchable. The relationships. LA. Coming home. The ICU. The LVAD. All of it. Nobody handles this shit the way I can. Not because I'm special in the way people mean when they say that. But because this specific combination of fire and faith and long suffering and stubbornness was built for exactly this load. I wouldn't wish this on anyone. Not even my worst enemies. But I wouldn't have it any other way. Because I know I've helped people just by how I move through it. Just by living. Just by surviving with my head up and my chest out.

There is beauty in that. That's the beauty in the struggle. And if the price of becoming someone who can help the world just by being himself is everything I've been through then I paid the right price and I'd pay it again.

People often tell me they forget what I'm facing.

I've talked about it openly and answered questions honestly when asked. But I've never led with it. Never walked into a room needing people to see my struggle before they could see me. Never let what I'm going through become the first thing I introduce about myself.

The world sees how I carry myself and forgets what I'm carrying. People see the grace and assume it comes free. It doesn't. There are mornings when the weight is present before I even open my eyes. Days when carrying it quietly requires more than I feel like I have. Moments when the performance of okay would be so much easier than the practice of actually being okay.

But I make the choice anyway. Not to perform strength. Because I refuse to let what I'm going through become who I am.

People who've watched Grey's Anatomy know a character named Denny Duquette. A man with a serious heart condition who became the most alive, most loving, most fully present person in every room he entered. Not because he pretended everything was fine. But because he made a decision about who he was going to be regardless of what his body was doing. He led with love and grace and a genuine aliveness that made everyone around him feel more present just by being near him.

To be fully here, lead with love, and let what I'm carrying deepen me instead of diminish me.

That choice is available to you too. Not as performance. As practice. As the daily decision to be more than what's happening to you.

Pain taught me something nothing else could have. Humility. The bone deep kind that comes from having your body stop doing what you always assumed it would do. From realizing that the control you thought you had over your life, your health, your future, your timeline, was always more limited than you believed.

I thought I was in control, moving at full speed, strong, confident, convinced that my will and my work ethic were the primary forces shaping my life. I had built an identity around being the person who made things happen. Who led. Who figured it out.

Then my body introduced me to the truth. You are not Superman. You never were.

Having that confidence stripped away by something you couldn't hustle your way out of, couldn't outwork, couldn't charm or strategize around, that was humbling in a way that reached places nothing else had ever touched.

Looking back I can say it plainly now. I needed that.

Made me more present. More honest. A version of me that stopped performing like he had it all figured out.

Pain made me human in ways that success never could have. And then it did something I didn't see coming.

I don't have my own children. That's a truth I've had to sit with in a way that doesn't get easier just because you've accepted it. There's a version of my future I always imagined that included being a father, having kids of my own, passing something down to them. Whether that happens is in God's hands. I've made my peace with that. But the desire for it, the love I have available for children who aren't here yet, that didn't go anywhere. It just needed somewhere to go.

So I created the Fueled by Love Foundation.

For the last four years, regardless of what has been happening in my life, I have shown up for the children of a local elementary school. School supply drives. Toy drives. Book fair events. Showing up with something to give and nothing to prove. Stranger to most of them. Consistent to all of them.

There have been years where showing up required more than I had. Where the financial situation was pressing. Where my health was uncertain. Where the last thing I had to spare was time or energy or resources. I showed up anyway. Because those kids have their entire future ahead of them and I believe with everything in me that one stranger who shows up consistently and positively can help shape what that future looks like. What they believe is possible. What they understand about being seen and valued and loved by someone who didn't have to show up but chose to.

I come back to Lockhart Elementary at different moments throughout the year. Different events, different seasons, different reasons to show up. And every time I walk through those doors something happens that still catches me off guard even though it's happened more than once now.

The kids remember me.

Not just a vague recognition. They run up to me. They hug me. They tell me about school. They show me their new sneakers like I'm someone who would genuinely want to see them, and I do. They remind me of specific toys I gave them like the memory is fresh even when months have passed. At an age where everything is new and everything is competing for their attention, they held onto something I gave them and they held onto me.

The faculty and staff have told me directly that they count on me. That they look forward to when I'm coming back. That what I've built with that school over these four years means something to the people inside it.

I don't take that lightly. There's a difference between being appreciated and being counted on. Appreciation is warm. Being counted on is weight. Good weight. The kind that gives you a reason to show up even on the days when showing up costs you something.

When I'm standing in that hallway and a kid grabs my hand or shows me something they're proud of, I feel like I matter. Love moving in both directions at once. Peace that doesn't come from anywhere else in my life. I don't go looking for those moments. They just find me every time I show up. This past year's toy drive I brought my little cousin Adam with me and had him wear a Santa Claus suit to add to it. Adam is 19 and skinny as hell so he looked less like Santa Claus and more like Santa YN, you know, Santa young nigga, but he showed up for me and suited up anyway and that meant everything. So Adam and I are standing in the middle of the auditorium cracking jokes, gifts spread out across tables in different sections, kids walking around browsing for what they want. We're in our own little world for a minute just laughing at the situation when I notice this little kid across the room just staring at us. Not waving, not smiling, just grilling us with a full mean mug like he's trying to figure something out. I nudge Adam like you see this little man over here? We watch him for a minute and then he just starts walking toward us, still with the same face, serious as hell. He walks right up, looks at both of us, and then just hugs Adam's Santa YN suit and hugs me. No buildup. No fanfare. Just a hug. And then he looks up at me and says you came last year too. I said yeah I did. And just like that he turned around and ran off like he had somewhere important to be. I stood there for a second after he left and didn't say anything. That kid didn't need a speech. He didn't need an explanation of why I show up. He just needed to know I came back.

And I did. That's what four years of showing up builds and I wouldn't trade it for anything.

That foundation, that love, that showing up, none of it would exist without the pain.

The health situation cracked me open, damn near like they cracked open my chest to put this shit in. The uncertainty about my own future softened something in me that used to be harder. The possibility that I might not have my own children redirected a love that had nowhere else to go directly into the lives of children who needed it. Pain didn't just take from me. It produced something in me that I then got to give away.

Pain didn't just work on me in that season. It worked through me, into the lives of children who have no idea what I'm carrying when I walk through that door.

My grace is sufficient for you, for my power is made perfect in weakness.

— 2 Corinthians 12:9

Not despite weakness. In it. Through it.

This is not a consolation prize for people who couldn't avoid difficulty. It's a fundamental truth about how real strength actually works. The places where you are most broken, most humbled, most stripped of the illusion of control, those are precisely the places where grace gets access to you.

You cannot receive what you're too strong to need.

Pain has a way of making you need things you would have otherwise refused. Humility. Help. Faith. The kind of presence that only comes from having been brought low enough to understand what actually matters. The kind of grace that only arrives when you've finally stopped pretending you don't need it.

That's the beginning of real strength, and I'm still learning that. Pain is not a one time teacher. It keeps showing up with new lessons at new depths, and each time it does I have a choice. Fight it or learn from it. Close off or open up. Let it make me smaller or let it make me more.

I'm choosing more. Every time. Even when more is harder than less.

It ain't about how hard you hit. It's about how hard you can get hit and keep moving forward.

— Rocky Balboa, Rocky Balboa

That line has never left me. About the capacity to absorb what life throws at you, feel the full weight of it, and keep moving anyway.

The hit is real. Pain is real. What it takes from you is real. But your life, the actual quality and depth and meaning of it, is not determined by whether you get hit. It's determined by what you do after.

Pain does not come with a fixed meaning. The meaning is yours to assign.

You can decide that pain is punishment. That it's evidence of life's cruelty. That it has targeted you specifically and the only honest response is bitterness or resignation. Some days that feeling is real and valid and it deserves its space.

Or you can decide that pain is preparation. That it's stripping away what was never meant to stay. Producing humility where arrogance lived. Building depth where comfort had kept things shallow. Introducing you to a version of yourself that the easy path never would have required you to become.

It shows you what you're made of when the performance falls away. Who shows up when showing up costs something. What actually matters once everything else has been stripped.

What gets revealed in those moments, the character, the faith, the love, the resilience, the humility, belongs to you now. Permanently. No circumstance can revoke it. No future hardship can take it back. It was produced in the fire and it will hold in the fire.

And sometimes it takes something from you, something you wanted deeply and may never have, and transforms that loss into a love so specific and so directed that it changes the lives of people who never even knew what it cost you to show up for them.

That version of you is worth every hard thing it took to find.

Show up anyway. And when you show up you're going to discover something about yourself that the hard season was building the whole time.

Chapter 5 — You Don't Look Like What You've Been Through

Survive through the drought, find the beauty in the struggle.

— J. Cole

There is a version of strength that nobody teaches you about. The kind that comes from being hit and deciding how you carry it.

People see you and think they know your story.

They see how you carry yourself. The way you walk into a room. The energy you bring. They build a version of your life in their head based on what's visible, what's presented, what made it through the filter before it reached them. Most of the time they're wrong.

What people see is the edited version. The one that made it through. The one that learned how to carry weight without announcing it. Someone who decided somewhere along the way that survival didn't have to look like suffering even when suffering was exactly what was happening.

You don't look like what you've been through, and that isn't luck, that's the kind of strength that only gets built by deciding how you carry what life puts on you.

I wear a fanny pack every day.

Inside that pack is the LVAD controller and batteries. Most people walking past me have no idea.

Most people don't know that when they first see me. They see a guy in his forties with a fanny pack and they think what they think. Then they talk to me or they watch me move or they see me in the gym and something shifts. The story they assumed doesn't match the person in front of them.

There's a scar running down the center of my chest. Visible when I take my shirt off. Evidence of everything my body has been through. When people ask about it I sometimes let them put their ear to my chest to hear these fucking 808s and heartbreaks with the damn LVAD humming.

That sound, steady and mechanical, is the sound of my life continuing. Most days now I forget it's even there. The thing keeping me alive has become so much a part of my daily existence that there are moments it just disappears into the background.

That's not denial or performance. That's the human capacity to keep living fully even inside extraordinary circumstances. Adaptation.

About a year after receiving the LVAD I was getting back into the gym seriously. Reclaiming something that had felt like it was slipping away. A friend named Moe asked me to come to Alphaland to record some content. I decided that day was going to be my announcement. Not with words. Just with presence. Showing up. Lifting. Going shirtless. Letting people see exactly what I was working with and working through simultaneously.

That gym was busy. I got stares. What happened after the stares is what I remember most.

People came up to me one after another. Wanting to understand. Wanting to know how. Looking at the scar and the machine and then looking at what I was doing and trying to reconcile the two. What I saw in their faces wasn't pity.

It was permission.

You can still move. Still show up. Still be yourself even when your body is working against you.

That day wasn't about proving something to the world. It was about showing the world what refusing to be defined looks like in real time.

We live in a time where struggle can become an identity. Where pain becomes content. Where people build platforms off what they're going through. I'm not knocking it. Survival looks different for everyone.

But I made a decision early on that I was never going to lead with what was wrong with me. Never going to let my condition be my introduction.

I didn't want a life that depended on me staying broken. I didn't want a community that came for my suffering and had nowhere to go when I got better. I didn't want to look up one day and realize the only story I had left to tell was the one about what my body was going through.

If I'm being honest that choice probably cost me. Financially. In visibility. There are people with similar stories who built larger platforms specifically because they leaned into the struggle as content.

No regrets. What I built instead is something that can't be taken away when the health situation changes. An identity that isn't dependent on staying sick. A community that came for who I am not what I'm surviving.

That's worth more than any platform built on suffering. Sometimes carrying it gracefully means carrying it alone.

There are moments where I wish people actually remembered. Not for sympathy or handouts. Just to feel like the weight I carry daily is seen even when I'm not showing it. The world sees how I carry myself and forgets what I'm carrying.

That line lives in me because it's true in a way that's hard to explain to someone who hasn't experienced it. The same grace that makes people forget what I'm facing can make them take for granted what it costs to show up the way I show up. To be consistent when consistency requires more than they know. To smile genuinely when smiling requires choosing it consciously.

Your grace is not evidence that you're fine. It's evidence of your character.

My brother Nick was one of the strongest people I've ever known. We didn't call him Nick. We called him Big Nick.

Six feet something. Close to four hundred pounds. A presence that filled a room before he said a word. Hard as nails on the outside in the way that men from a certain generation learned to be, but underneath that he was a giant teddy bear. Soft as Charmin. The kind of man whose size made you feel safe just being near him.

There was a significant age gap between us which meant that when I was little I didn't fully understand what to call what he was to me. Brother didn't feel like enough for what he represented. So I called him my best bud. A little kid's way of saying this person is my person. This is who I feel safest with. This is who I want to be around.

As we all got older Big Nick became something else to the family. He became the one you called. Not just for emergencies. For everything. If Mike and I were beefing with each other we'd both separately pick up the phone and call Nick to vent about the other one. He'd listen to both sides, hold the weight of both of us, and somehow make each of us feel heard without betraying the other. He was a counselor before anyone called him that. A mediator. A safe place.

The whole family ran through Nick, and when you have someone like that in your life you don't fully appreciate what they're doing until they're not there to do it anymore. You don't realize how much you've been leaning on something until it's gone and you feel the full weight of what you were resting on.

In the months before he passed, after his stroke, I watched him in that hospital. Watched the fight in him. Watched a man that size try to hold onto something that was slipping away no matter how hard he gripped it. I remember one of the last things he told me. He said he was tired.

I've carried that word with me ever since. Not as grief exactly. As reverence for what it means to reach the end of your fight. To have given everything and feel the weight of having given everything. Big Nick fought hard and long and with everything he had. When he finally said he was tired it wasn't weakness. It was a man who had left nothing on the field.

I'm tired too sometimes. I'll say that here in a way I struggle to say it out loud anywhere else. Here's what I know about my tired that was different from Nick's.

His fight was ending. Mine isn't. There's a fear I carry quietly, that saying I'm tired out loud means something it doesn't actually mean. Like naming the weight gives it permission to win.

Naming the weight isn't surrendering to it. I'm tired. And I ain't quitting.

Both of those things are completely true at the same time, and holding them together isn't contradiction. It's perseverance. The kind that looks at it clearly, feels the full weight of it, and chooses to keep moving anyway.

Nick fought until he couldn't fight anymore, and I'm going to do the same.

The role Nick played in our family, the one everybody called, the counselor, the safe place, the person who held space for everyone else's weight without making it about himself, I've somehow stepped into that without anyone officially passing it to me. Friends call me. Family calls me. People going through hard things find their way to me and I find myself doing what Nick did. Listening. Holding it. Making people feel heard without judgment.

I didn't plan that. I didn't apply for it. But I think about Nick and I think there are worse things to become than the person he was. If carrying his legacy means being the one people feel safe enough to call then I'll carry it as long as I'm here.

The losses shaped me. The grief changed me. Watching my brothers fight and lose their fights changed something in me permanently.

I'm tired.

And I ain't quitting.

That's not just mine. Somebody reading this knows exactly what that combination feels like. Who was your Big Nick?

Who was your Big Nick? Who was the person everybody ran to? The one who held space for everyone else without ever asking for anything in return? The one whose absence left a gap so specific you still feel the shape of it?

And the harder question is who have you become because of them? What role have you quietly stepped into that nobody officially handed you? What parts of them are you carrying forward in the way you show up for the people in your life?

The people who shaped us don't just leave us with grief when they go. They leave us with capacity. A blueprint for how to show up. A standard for what it looks like to be the person a whole family runs to.

You don't have to have it all figured out to carry that forward. You just have to be willing to show up the way they showed up for you.

You are not your wound, not your diagnosis, not your loss, not your worst season or the weight you carry or the scar it left.

You are the person still here after all of it. Still here means the story isn't finished.

You don't look like what you've been through, which means it didn't define you. You did. Knowing that doesn't mean the question stops coming. It just means you have a choice about how long you let it stay.

Chapter 6 — Stop Asking "Why Me?"

When we are no longer able to change a situation, we are challenged to change ourselves.

— Viktor Frankl

Maybe you've asked it.

Why me. Why this. Why now.

Most people have. And most people never say it out loud because asking it feels like weakness. Like you're admitting the weight is winning. Like voicing the question gives it permission to be true. So it stays internal, quiet, running in the background of everything while you try to function on top of it.

I understand the question. I'm not here to shame anyone for asking it. When something unfair lands on you, when you look around and see people living unbothered while you're carrying something that feels like it was targeted specifically at you, the question rises up almost automatically. It's human. It's the mind trying to make sense of something that doesn't make sense.

I've lived with that question sitting on my chest and I can tell you what it does.

It faces backward, living in the past, in blame, in the search for an explanation that will never be satisfying enough to justify what it costs you to keep looking for it. And while you're facing backward, life keeps moving forward without you.

You cannot build forward while facing backward.

Nothing about that answer changes what actually happened. The loss is still the loss.

The answer to why me has never once moved anyone forward. I don't ask it, not because my situation doesn't justify the question, not because the weight isn't heavy enough to earn some real anger at the universe, but because I figured something out early that has protected me in ways I can't fully calculate.

It's okay to have a bad moment. Feel it. Sit in it. Let it be real. But you have to move on.

A bad moment you never close becomes a bad hour. Then a bad week. Then one day you look up and realize you've been living a bad life and you never made a single decision to do that.

That progression is not dramatic. It's quiet. It happens slowly in the background while you're still technically functioning. You're still going to work, still showing up, still doing what needs to be done. But underneath all of it the why me question is running, adding weight to everything, coloring every new experience with the grief of the one you never processed and moved through.

That's how people get stuck, not in one dramatic moment of giving up, but in the slow accumulation of bad moments they never gave themselves permission to close.

I feel things deeply. I want to be clear about that because this is not about suppressing emotion or performing strength or pretending that hard things don't hurt. They do. I cry. I get angry. I sit in the weight of things sometimes and let it be exactly as heavy as it is.

And then I turn the page, because that thing, whatever it is, cannot be my story. It's a part of my story. There's a difference between a chapter and the whole book. The LVAD is a part of my story. The losses are a part of my story. The financial pressure, the uncertainty, the waiting, all of it is a part of my story. But none of it is the whole story and I refuse to let any single part of it write the final word about who I am and what my life means.

The connection between how you feel mentally and emotionally and what happens to you physically is not a theory. It's not a wellness trend or something people say on motivational posters. It is science. Stress, grief, anxiety, depression, when they are prolonged and unaddressed they do real measurable damage to the human body. They affect your heart, your immune system, your hormones, your ability to heal.

For most people that's an interesting fact. For me it's survival, not a metaphor, not a mindset concept. Actual survival.

I have an LVAD running and a transplant that hasn't come yet. I cannot afford to let stress and grief and the weight of unanswered questions sit in my body unchecked. The mental and emotional and the physical are not separate systems. They are connected. What you carry in your mind and your heart shows up in your body whether you invited it to or not. The gym became something different for me because of this. I've always loved it but now it's a sanctuary. Headphones in, the rest of the world completely gone. Whatever was sitting on my chest when I walked in starts to move. I'm not in my head about the transplant timeline or the financial pressure or any of the things I can't control from inside a weight room. I'm just there. In my body. Doing something that's entirely in my hands. That's not just a workout. For me that's medicine.

So when I say I refuse to stay in the why me question it is not because I'm spiritually advanced or because I've figured out some secret to positivity. It's because I understand on a level most people fortunately don't have to understand that the things I allow to live in me have a direct relationship to whether I keep living.

That urgency is mine specifically. But the truth behind it belongs to everyone.

You are trying to live too. Maybe not in the same immediate physical way. But every day you spend stuck in the why me question is a day you're not fully alive. Every year the bad moment bleeds into is a year you didn't get to live the way you were built to live.

Viktor Frankl survived the worst conditions a human being can endure. Inside a Nazi concentration camp he lost everything and still came back with one of the most powerful truths ever written.

When we are no longer able to change a situation we are challenged to change ourselves.

Not cursed. Not punished. Challenged.

A challenge asks something from you. A curse just leaves you waiting for someone to lift it. Those two words sitting in the same situation produce completely different lives.

Frankl had every reason to ask why me. He chose his response instead. That freedom, the freedom to choose how you respond to what you cannot change, is still available to you right now in whatever you're facing.

Acknowledging it fully and refusing to let it be the final destination. That's the move.

You can acknowledge where you are without deciding it's where you'll stay.

My first birthday after the surgery I was six months post-op with the LVAD and back in the gym, back at the tattoo shop, back in these streets, back to flirting, just back to living life. We had come back from a day party, the whole crew, and there was a birthday cake and everyone was giving little toasts. That's when my older cousin Paul said his piece. Told me how strong I was. Said he had been watching me handle everything and couldn't believe how I moved through it. Said I handled it like a G. That moment stuck with me not because of the compliment but because of what it revealed. My grace had confused people. They had been watching for something that never came. There is also a quiet social pressure around suffering that nobody talks about openly. People expect a certain performance of pain from you. A certain level of visible devastation that confirms for them that what you went through was significant. When you don't deliver that performance, when you move through it with more grace than they anticipated, they don't always know what to do with you.

Sometimes the hardest part isn't going through it. It's going through it differently than people expected you to.

You don't owe anyone a performance of your pain. Your healing doesn't require an audience.

The better question has always been what now.

What now is the only question that actually moves you. It looks at the full weight of where you are and still points forward. Puts you back in the driver's seat without pretending the road wasn't rough to get here.

Think about where you are right now. Whatever you're carrying. Whatever question has been running in the background of your life. Is it facing forward or backward? Is it building something or keeping you stuck in something that has already happened and cannot be changed?

The bad moment is allowed to be real. Feel it. Honor it. Don't rush past it. Then close it. Turn the page.

Because your story is still being written and the "why me" chapter is not the one worth spending your life in.

Stop asking why me. Ask what now. Then go build something.

Chapter 7 — For Every Dark Night

Through every dark night there's a bright day after that. So no matter how hard it get, stick your chest out, keep your head up, and handle it.

— Tupac Shakur

Have you ever been in a moment where something outside of you confirmed everything you'd been believing on the inside?

Something you didn't ask for or plan, that just showed up and settled something in you that didn't have a word yet.

That happened to me. And the way it happened matters because it wasn't dramatic or calculated or the result of years of faithful church attendance. It was ordinary. Almost accidental. Which is exactly why I believe it was anything but.

My friend Hannah had been watching my Instagram lives. Something in what she was seeing moved her to reach out and invite me to church. I said yes with every intention of flaking. I didn't even set an alarm. That was on purpose. My plan was to sleep through it, apologize later, and keep moving.

But I woke up early.

I just woke up, fully awake, way before I needed to be, and no matter what I did I could not make myself go back to sleep. When Hannah called that morning I was already dressed with nowhere else to be.

So I went.

I walked into a church for the first time in twenty five years. And the pastor was preaching Job.

I sat in that room and felt something settle in me that I didn't have language for in the moment. Not emotion exactly. Something deeper and quieter than emotion. A recognition. Like something I had been carrying for years without being able to name it had just been handed back to me with a label on it. It was confirmation.

For years people had been telling me I reminded them of Job. People who knew my story, who had watched how I moved through what I was carrying, kept coming back to the same name. Job. I had heard enough about his story to understand why they were making the connection but I had never sat in a room and heard it preached with the full weight it deserved.

That morning I did, and everything I had believed, everything I had leaned on through the hardest seasons of my life without being able to fully articulate it or defend it, landed differently. The faith I had been carrying without religion, without the structure most people associate with belief, had been pointing me in the right direction the whole time.

I didn't plan that morning. I tried to avoid it. And it found me anyway.

That's what I mean when I say I know in my heart that I am exactly where I am supposed to be. As the deepest conviction I carry. That the path has been intentional even when it didn't look intentional from the inside.

Job was not a man who had done anything to deserve what happened to him. That's the first thing to understand. He wasn't being punished. He wasn't reaping what he had sown in some karmic sense. By every measure he was a righteous man living a good life. And then everything was stripped away, his children, his health, his wealth, his stability, everything that gave his life its shape and meaning dismantled in a season that offered no explanation.

The people closest to him, the ones who were supposed to be his support, showed up and made it worse. They told him he must have done something to deserve it. That there was no point holding on. That the only honest response to what was happening was to curse God and give up.

Job refused.

Not because he wasn't in pain. He was. He asked hard questions. He expressed real anger. He did not perform faith or pretend the suffering wasn't happening. He sat in the full weight of what was happening to him and still refused to let it be the final word.

What came at the end of his story was restoration and a depth of understanding that only that specific path could have produced. But here's what matters. From inside the suffering he couldn't see any of that. He wasn't holding on because he had a preview of the ending. He was holding on because letting go wasn't something he was willing to do regardless of what it cost him.

Job's story is not a story about suffering. It's a story about what holding on produces when you refuse to let the darkness write the final word about your life.

Faith doesn't always feel the way most people think it does. Most people picture faith as certainty, a settled knowing that everything is going to be fine, and then they compare that image to what they actually feel in their hardest moments and conclude that what they have isn't faith because it doesn't feel like that. Sometimes faith feels like continuing anyway when certainty has left the building. Like getting up on a Tuesday when Tuesday has nothing to recommend it. Like believing in a morning you cannot see from inside a night that has gone on longer than you thought you could survive.

Every day is hard for me. I'm not rich. I'm not famous. I have a life or death health situation that is ongoing and unresolved. There is nothing about my external circumstances that makes faith easy or obvious or the path of least resistance.

And every single morning I wake up grateful that I woke up. That's where it starts. Before anything around me confirms that today is going to be different.

Just gratitude for being here. Then a decision. A quiet, deliberate, completely unsupported by evidence decision that today is going to be amazing. The break is coming. The heart is coming. My purpose is unfolding exactly the way it's supposed to.

I believe it before anything in my day confirms it. Before the phone rings. Before anything shifts. Just the moment my eyes open.

None of that is naivety, none of it is blind optimism or spiritual performance or telling yourself lies to get through the day. It's what faith actually looks like from the inside on an ordinary Tuesday.

The first time I heard the words for every dark night there is a bright day I wasn't in church. I was listening to Tupac.

Something in the rawness of how he carried both his pain and his belief made that line land in a place it has never left. Tupac wasn't polished or perfect. He was a man in real conflict. Real darkness. Real struggle that he never fully resolved. And he believed anyway. Loudly. Imperfectly. Without pretense.

That's the kind of faith I understand, not the kind that looks clean from the outside, not the kind that arrives after everything works out and you can reflect on it with the luxury of hindsight, but the kind that holds on in the middle of something real because letting go is simply not an option you're willing to accept.

There's a scene in The Dark Knight Rises where Bruce Wayne is at the bottom of a pit. Broken. He tries to climb out over and over and fails every time because he has a rope around him. A safety net that catches him when he falls.

Someone tells him the truth. Climb without the rope.

Not because the rope is wrong. Because the rope was removing the one thing the climb required. Full commitment. The kind that only exists when falling means actually falling. When there is no safety net between you and the consequence of not making it.

Bruce removes the rope and climbs out. Real faith works the same way. It's not the safety net. It's the climb without one. The moment you stop hedging. Stop operating from fear of what happens if it doesn't work and start operating from the certainty that it will.

When faith becomes your only option it stops being a feeling and starts being a force.

I removed my rope a long time ago, and every morning I wake up grateful and decide today is going to be amazing and believe the break is coming without a single guarantee that it is. Climbing without the rope. Choosing life and life only as the only direction worth moving in.

If you're in the middle of a night that has gone on too long, if you've been holding on and praying and doing everything right and the morning still hasn't arrived in the form you hoped for, hear this.

The morning is not a metaphor.

It comes without fail. Without exception. Regardless of how long or how complete the night was. The sun rises every single day not because the darkness deserved to end but because light is what comes after dark. Always. Without negotiation.

Your morning is coming, not on your schedule, not in the form you expected, but it is coming and the question is not whether it arrives. The question is whether you're still here when it does.

What's being built in you while you wait, the depth, the faith, the capacity to hold on when holding on costs everything, that becomes who you are. Job was not the same man at the end of his story that he was at the beginning. The suffering produced something in him that the comfortable version of his life never could have reached.

The same is true for you. Whatever you're in right now is not the whole story. The night is real. The weight is real. The length of it is real and I'm not asking you to pretend otherwise.

Just don't let it write the final word. Hold on.

For every dark night there is a bright day, and I stopped hearing that as a lyric a long time ago because I've lived it enough times to know it's a promise. Holding onto that gets easier when you learn to loosen your grip on everything else.

Chapter 8 — Control What You Can, Release What You Can't

God grant me the serenity to accept the things I cannot change, the courage to change the things I can, and the wisdom to know the difference.

— The Serenity Prayer

There is something in your life right now that you know you can't control but you haven't fully let go of yet.

You know what it is. You don't need anyone to name it for you. It sits in a specific place in your chest and you feel it most in the quiet moments when there's nothing left to distract you from it.

For me it's not the health situation. I've made a kind of peace with the uncertainty there. It took years and it cost me things I'm still paying for in quiet ways. But I found it.

Being single. The relationship I haven't found yet. A family. Kids. Something to leave behind that breathes and carries my name and knows I was here. Those are the things I find myself gripping most tightly. The outcomes I want most deeply that are furthest outside my control no matter what I do or how hard I work toward them. Some nights that's the only thing in the room with me. Not the LVAD. Not the transplant list. Just that specific absence. The version of my life I haven't gotten to live yet. And I let myself feel the full weight of it because pretending it's not there never made it smaller.

I say that plainly because I think most people have a version of this. The thing they intellectually know they can't force but emotionally can't fully release. The want that sits in the chest and refuses to be reasoned away no matter how much perspective you accumulate or how many times you remind yourself to be grateful.

That's the exhaustion nobody talks about honestly, not the exhaustion from doing too much, but the exhaustion from gripping outcomes that don't belong in your hands. From spending your energy on the gap between what you want and what is. From trying through sheer force of will to close that gap yourself when closing it was never in your hands to begin with.

It's the exhaustion of trying to win a fight you were never meant to control. You can be doing everything right and still waiting.

You can be showing up every day, working with full intention, not hurting anyone, moving in the right direction, being exactly who you're supposed to be, and the thing you want most still hasn't arrived.

That tension is real. And it's one of the most disorienting feelings a person can carry because it defies the logic we're taught. We're taught that if you do the right things the right outcomes follow. And sometimes they do. But sometimes you do everything right and you still wait. And the waiting doesn't mean you're doing something wrong. It just means the outcome isn't yours to control.

So I pull back. Get quiet. Stop measuring my life against the thing I'm still waiting on and start looking honestly at the small wins. The little steps. The quiet evidence that things are moving even when the big thing hasn't arrived yet.

That shift in focus is harder than it sounds. It requires a real decision to be present in your actual life instead of living in the gap between where you are and where you want to be. But when you can genuinely sit in gratitude for what has already shown up, not as a performance of contentment but as a real acknowledgment that progress is happening even when the destination isn't visible yet, something in you settles.

You can want more and be grateful for what you have at the same time. Those two things are not in conflict. Holding both of them simultaneously is not settling. It's wisdom.

Marcus Aurelius wrote something that functions like a map. You have power over your mind, not outside events.

Releasing control in my daily life looks like going to the gym. Two, three, four hours sometimes just being in my body, out of my head, away from the worry and the waiting. Just the work. The weight. The physical reality of what my body can still do even with everything it's been through. There's a clarity that comes from that space. A return to what's actually in my hands right now.

It looks like creating content that makes me laugh. Finding something funny in the middle of hard things. Not performance. Survival. The deliberate choice to access lightness when gravity is pulling hard.

It looks like going to family. Because tomorrow isn't promised for any of us and the people who love you unconditionally, even when you're just present and quiet and together, are one of the most powerful reminders that the most important things in your life are not the things you're waiting on. They're already here.

And then there are the plants.

But before I get to the plants I have to tell you about Houston. Because Houston is the surrender story. I used to think coming back here was temporary. Like a detour. Something to move through before I got back to the life I had been building in LA. Even after the hospital stays I kept thinking I would bounce back, get my health right, and return to where I was supposed to be. It wasn't until the days after the LVAD surgery, lying still for the first time in years, that something in me finally let go of that idea. Not because I gave up. Because I understood for the first time that Houston wasn't where life had trapped me. It was where I had been led. Not forced. Led. And looking at this from honest eyes I can see it was always supposed to be this way. Surrender doesn't feel like losing. It feels like finally stopping the argument with something that was already true.

What started as a couple of gifts and a few impulse purchases at the grocery store has turned into close to a hundred plants. Tropical houseplants. Corms and cuttings I've grown into entirely new plants. A whole living world I've been quietly learning and tending and watching thrive.

There are mornings I wake up and the first thing I do before I check my phone, before I think about the transplant list or the finances or any of the things I can't move on yet, is walk through and check on them. See what's new. See what's pushing out another leaf overnight like it didn't get the memo that things are hard right now. There's one in particular that I keep coming back to. A Monstera Thai Constellation I stumbled upon at Cornelius Nursery in Houston. I wasn't looking for it. I just found it and something said pay attention. There were five or six of them that day and I spent a solid 45 minutes going back and forth between them, checking the leaves, comparing the variegation, taking pictures and sending them to an AI to help me evaluate which one was actually the healthiest. Forty five minutes over a houseplant. I'm aware of how that sounds. But I had decided I was going to do this right and I wasn't spending $69 on the wrong one. I finally just said fuck it, picked the best one, and walked it to the register. The woman scanned it and told me it was 30 percent off because of that weekend's sale. I hadn't known. I just showed up, did my part, made the best decision I could with what I had, and let the rest work itself out. A plant taught me that. I can't even lie, that shit still makes me smile. It's been growing ever since, constantly, lush and full in a way that still catches me off guard some mornings when I walk past it. I learned about moss poles, did my research, put one in to give it something to climb, and now it reaches up with new growth coming in almost every week like it has somewhere to be. By the end of the year that plant is going to fill a corner of this room the way those giant TikTok plant creator plants do that everybody stops scrolling for. I know exactly where it started. I watched every inch of it get here. I did something small and consistent and showed up for it and it responded. Somewhere in that I found something I needed more than I knew.

I know how that sounds coming from me. Honestly though I'm lowkey embracing this plant daddy shit. Turning into the plant whisperer. Swole ass dude standing in his apartment listening to Sade or Cleo Soul talking to his plants at 6am. Trust me I've caught my own reflection and thought the same thing. But here we are and the plants are thriving so I'm not stopping.

The plants taught me something I wasn't expecting. The heart comes when it comes. The relationship shows up when it shows up. None of that is in my hands no matter what I do.

But I can water a plant. I can take a cutting and give it the right conditions and watch something new grow from what was already there. I can nurture something living and see it respond. I can put my hands in soil and tend something and watch it thrive under my care.

A hundred plants taught me more about controlling what I can and releasing what I can't than almost anything else I've encountered, not because it's a small thing when everything else feels uncertain, but because it became the daily practice of focusing on what's actually in your hands. Of pouring your energy into what you can influence and releasing your grip on what you can't.

There's a reason that lesson keeps showing up in different forms across different traditions and different generations.

Trust in the Lord with all your heart and lean not on your own understanding.

— Proverbs 3:5

That last part has never left me.

My understanding, as hard earned as it is, is still limited. Still finite. Still working with incomplete information about outcomes I cannot see. Leaning on it exclusively means navigating an uncertain future with a map that only shows the ground beneath my current feet. At some point you have to acknowledge that the co-pilot has visibility you don't. And trusting that means loosening your grip on the wheel even when loosening your grip feels like losing.

Letting go of the outcome doesn't mean you stopped caring about it. You're still working. Still showing up. The difference is you stopped strangling it.

I still show up every day. Still doing everything within my power toward the outcomes I want, in the gym, building, writing this book, moving with full intention toward the life I believe is possible.

Effort without release becomes obsession. You grip so tightly that you strangle the thing you're trying to grow. Release without effort becomes passivity. You let go so completely that you stop doing your part. Together, effort and release produce the rarest combination there is.

A person who works like everything depends on them and rests like they know it doesn't.

And it's something you practice daily. Some days you find it. Some days the grip comes back and you have to consciously loosen it again. The practice is returning to it. Not arriving at it permanently.

Is it yours to carry? Or are you holding onto it because releasing it feels like giving up on something you want? Because there's a difference between those two things and it matters.

Responsibility says I will do everything in my power. Control says I will determine the outcome. One is yours. The other never was.

What are the small wins in your life right now that you've been overlooking because they're not the big thing you're waiting on? What's already here that deserves your gratitude while you keep believing for what's still coming?

Let me give you mine. The gym. With everything my body has been through, with everything still unresolved and uncertain, I am strong again. When you see me you see a man who lifts heavy, who grinds, who moves like someone who never stopped. That didn't happen by accident. It happened because when I couldn't control the transplant timeline or the financial situation or whether the relationship I want has arrived yet, I could control showing up to the gym. I could control the work. I could pour everything I had into something that was actually in my hands and watch it respond.

A small win that isn't small at all. Proof that the practice works. You focus on what's yours, you pour into what you can influence, and over time what you can influence starts to look like something worth being proud of.

Do your part completely. Be present for what's already here. Release the rest. And be still. In that stillness something becomes clear. The things you've been through weren't just yours to survive. They were yours to give.

What's your version of that?

Chapter 9 — Your Story Is Your Power

There is no greater agony than bearing an untold story inside you.

— Maya Angelou

Nobody told you that your story had value. Not the messy parts. Not the chapters you'd rather skip over or the version of yourself you had to leave behind to become who you are today.

Nobody sat you down and said what you've been through is not a liability. It's a gift.

Not necessarily to you, although it has shaped you in ways nothing else could. But to the person right now in the middle of something that feels exactly like what you've already survived. The person in the hospital room or the quiet apartment or the car in a parking lot somewhere trying to figure out how to keep going. The person who needs to know someone else has been where they are and found a way through.

Your story is their roadmap.

Withholding it out of shame or fear or pride is one of the most expensive choices you can make. For the people who needed what only you could give them and never got it because you decided your story wasn't worth sharing.

I had two brothers who saw something in me before I could fully see it in myself.

Nick and Jule. Both of them, separately, from the time I was young, told me the same thing in different ways. That I was a leader. A captain. A voice. A vision. That people were going to gravitate toward me in every space I entered and that it was my responsibility to understand what that meant and use it for something.

I heard them. I received it with gratitude. And then I smiled and kept moving because that's what humility looks like when you're not quite ready to fully claim what people keep seeing in you.

Over time I've had to sit with what that actually means. When two people who love you and know you deeply, who have watched you move through the world since you were a child, keep coming back to the same observation independently, it isn't flattery. It isn't brothers being generous with their little brother. It's two sets of eyes seeing something real that you're too close to see clearly yourself.

Nick and Jule were right. I know that now in a way I couldn't fully accept when they were here to say it.

There is something in me that people respond to. I didn't manufacture it. I didn't build it through strategy or positioning or carefully curated content. It's just there. In every room I walk into. Online and offline. With strangers and with people who have known me for years. People gravitate in a way that I stopped being able to explain away as coincidence a long time ago.

For years I didn't fully use it because I was hiding parts of myself that I thought would cost me.

The health situation. The losses. The reality of what I was carrying every single day behind the smile and the energy and the content. I presented something polished while carrying something much heavier underneath. And what kept me there wasn't just privacy.

Ego and pride. The quiet resistance to being fully seen

Who wants to deal with someone carrying what I'm carrying. Who signs up for that. Who stays once they really know.

That's what ego and pride do when they're running unchecked. They convince you that your realness is a liability. That your story is something to manage and minimize rather than something to offer. They keep you in the shadows performing a version of yourself that's easier for people to digest while the real version, the one with the actual depth and the actual proof, stays hidden.

I kept waiting for transparency to cost me. Every single time I had the courage to be honest the response was the opposite of what I feared. It wasn't pity or distance, it was connection, and that kept catching me off guard no matter how many times it happened.

Brené Brown spent years researching this and found what I was learning in real time. Vulnerability is not weakness. It's where real human connection is born.

People couldn't necessarily relate to the LVAD or the heart condition specifically. But they could relate to me. To carrying something heavy while still trying to function at full capacity. To being more than what you're going through even while you're going through it. To the fear that your real story would cost you the things you want most.

That fear is universal. Most people are just still letting it win.

When everything first happened with my health the outpouring of support humbled me in a way I wasn't prepared for. People I had never met. People who had found me through a post or a video or a mutual connection became deeply invested in my life and my outcome. Messages from strangers telling me they were praying for me. People checking in consistently. A level of care and concern that made no logical sense given that most of them had never been in the same room as me.

I didn't understand it at first. I genuinely didn't know why so many people cared, and then slowly I started to understand.

That gave me fuel in a season when I needed it most, deepened my faith, confirmed something I had been too humble to fully claim

People have been telling me for years that there is favor over me. That something is different about how I move through the world. I used to smile and say thank you and keep going because that's what you do when you're not sure you've fully earned the weight of what people are speaking over you.

But I believe it now. I know it to be true, and here's what I understand about where that favor came from. It didn't come despite what I've been through. It came because of it. The depth people feel when they're around me or watching me or reading what I write came from the fire. The authority in my voice when I talk about holding on and keeping faith came from having actually been in the dark and found something worth holding onto.

Without the story I'm just someone with something to say. With it I'm someone with proof, and proof changes people in ways that information never can.

Toni Morrison said if there's a book you want to read but it hasn't been written yet you must write it. That's why this book exists. Not because someone asked me to write it. Because I needed it to exist. I was in the middle of everything looking for something that spoke to what I was actually living and couldn't find it. Something written from inside the fire not after it. So I wrote it.

That's what your story asks of you too. Not necessarily a book. Something honest. Some real offering of what you've been through and what you found in the middle of it. Because the person who needs it can only get it from you. Nobody else has lived your specific combination of fire and survival.

The internet has taught me something about this that I didn't fully understand before. My audience is a mix of people who came for the fitness content, the lifestyle content, the humor, the random things I find interesting on any given day. But there is a significant number of people who found me specifically because of my personal story. Because something in what I was living resonated with something in what they were carrying. And by telling mine I've been helping them find permission to live in theirs. To stop hiding their own story because they're afraid of what it will cost them.

That's the thing about your story. You think it's about you. It's not. It never was. It's about the person who finds it at exactly the right moment and realizes they're not alone in what they've been carrying. That someone else has been where they are. That the thing they've been ashamed of or hiding or managing privately is the exact thing that could set someone else free if they were willing to bring it into the light.

Shame grows in secrecy. Your story brought into the light loses power over you and gains power for someone else.

The people who use their story most powerfully don't wait until they're fully healed. They share it from the middle of the process, while they're still figuring it out, because someone needs what they know now, not what they'll know eventually.

Your story told from exactly where you are right now is more powerful than the finished version you're waiting to have.

Stop waiting until it's over to let it mean something. Stop letting ego and pride keep you in the shadows when your light is exactly what someone else needs.

Your story isn't something to survive. It's something to give. And what makes you willing to give it, what makes you willing to stay open and keep showing up, has a name.

Chapter 10 — Love Is the Fuel, Not the Reward

You're off to great places. Today is your day.
Your mountain is waiting, so get on your way.

— Dr. Seuss, Oh, The Places You'll Go!

There is a calling over some people's lives that others can see long before the person carrying it can.

I still have the book. Tattered. Worn. Held together by thirty six years of being carried, opened, and returned to in moments that mattered most.

A first grade teacher named Ms. Fitzgerald gave it to me when I was six years old. A copy of Oh, The Places You'll Go! by Dr. Seuss. The way she handed it to me said more than the book ever could. Something in the gesture communicated you are going somewhere. I see it. I want you to know I see it.

I don't know if she knew what she was planting in me that day. I just know it never left. Thirty six years later that tattered book is still locked away. Still my bible. Still the template I measure my life against. A first grade teacher poured something into a six year old boy that has outlasted heart surgery, an LVAD, and every hard thing in between.

That's love. Not the romantic kind people spend years waiting on. The kind that reaches you early, before you've earned anything or done enough to justify being believed in.

The kind that sees something in you before you even have the capacity to see it in yourself. Before self doubt has had the chance to arrive. Before the world has had the chance to tell you what you can and cannot be.

That's the love that has fueled my whole life. Most people treat love like a destination.

The thing waiting at the end. The relationship. The arrival. That moment life finally comes together and delivers what you've been hoping for. So they move through their days in a kind of deficit. Operating from not yet. Waiting for the love that will finally make everything make sense before they fully commit to living.

Love has never worked that way for me. Love has been the fuel, never the finish line.

It's the reason I get up on days when getting up requires a conscious decision. The reason I still show up for people when showing up costs me something they can't see. The reason I keep building, creating, writing this book from inside a season that has pressed on me from every direction and given me every excuse to shut down.

I have people counting on me. People who look to me to show up. To smile. To lead. To keep being me on the days being me is harder than it looks. And I don't carry that as pressure. I carry it as fuel.

But the truth goes deeper than that. One of the things that fuels me most is something I don't talk about enough. It's the love I carry for the younger version of myself. The kid I used to be. The shy one. Popular in some ways but a loner in others. The kid with big dreams and aspirations that felt almost too large to say out loud. The one who had people around him who believed in him, protected him, looked out for him, spoke things over him before he had any real proof to show them.

That kid had something planted in him by people like Ms. Fitzgerald, by Nick and Jule, by everyone who saw something and said so.

To fulfill what people saw in him. To become what they believed was possible and not let those dreams die unexamined while I'm still here and still able to do something about it.

There is also a young woman named Maliyah.

She isn't my biological daughter. But she is mine in every way that actually counts. The ways built from showing up consistently, from choosing someone, from being present across years in a way that has nothing to do with obligation and everything to do with love.

She's a young woman now, growing into a young adult, becoming something remarkable in front of my eyes. And one of the quietest but most powerful motivations I carry is the need to be here to see it. To be the person she can call on when she needs someone. To watch her become the woman and the human being I already know she has in her.

Not a small thing to carry. Everything, actually.

For the six year old holding that book, the younger me who was seen before he had proof, every version of me that someone poured into before I understood what they were building.

I owe winning and living to Ms. Fitzgerald and every person who believed in me before I had done anything to deserve it.

That debt doesn't feel like obligation. It feels like purpose.

James Baldwin wrote that love takes off the masks we fear we cannot live without.

That hits differently when you know what it is to live behind one. When the version people see is cleaner than the one you're actually carrying. When the outside is composed but the inside is heavy. When you've gotten so good at presenting strength that people forget to check on you.

Real love makes the mask unnecessary. It doesn't need the polished version. Doesn't wait until you're easier to hold. It sees you clearly and stays.

Some of the deepest love I've received didn't come in the form I expected. It came from a first grade teacher. From brothers who shaped me before I knew I was being shaped. From a community that formed around nothing more complicated than showing up honestly. From a young woman who calls me when she needs someone and trusts that I'll be there. From the inner child in me that kept believing even when the adult version was tired.

That love didn't show up at the end as a reward for getting life right. It showed up early. Sometimes quietly. Sometimes in ways I didn't understand until much later.

One day I looked back and realized it had been carrying me the whole time.

Love bears all things, believes all things, hopes all things, endures all things.

— 1 Corinthians 13:7

Not love as a feeling you fall into when conditions are favorable.

Not love as a feeling you fall into when conditions are favorable. Love as endurance. The force that keeps you moving when logic has run out and certainty has left the building. The thing underneath your whole life that refuses to let you stop even when stopping would be easier.

The love I understand now isn't the version the movies sold me. It's the version I've actually lived.

I don't have my person yet. I'm not writing from the other side of a love story that worked out. The romantic love I've been hoping for hasn't arrived in the form I want it yet.

And I am fueled by love every single day.

Community. Family. Purpose. Faith. The life I'm still building. The love I carry for the young woman who calls me hers even though biology didn't make it so. A love I carry for the kid I used to be and the promise I made to him without knowing I was making it. The love I have for the person I'm still becoming. That matters because it means I stopped waiting for love to begin my life.

My life is already moving on love, already carried by it, already being built by it. If the romantic love I've been hoping for arrives it won't be rescuing a life that hasn't started yet. It will be arriving into a life that was already fueled.

Where has love already shown up that you keep overlooking because it didn't arrive in the form you wanted most? Who believed in you early? Who saw something in you before there was evidence? Who gave you something that kept working in your life long after the moment itself passed?

And what about the younger version of you? The kid who had dreams before the world got complicated. The one who needed someone to show up and someone did. What did that version of you believe was possible before life started negotiating with those beliefs?

And if you've been pouring it outward for years without keeping any of it for yourself, you already know what that costs.

Chapter 11 — You Have to Choose Yourself

You do not have to set yourself on fire to keep others warm.

— Nayyirah Waheed

There is a version of yourself you put on hold.

Maybe it was for someone else, or for the right time that never came, or fear dressed up as patience. Whatever it was, at some point you stopped moving toward what you wanted.

I know that feeling personally. I moved to Los Angeles for a dream.

Not vaguely. Specifically. To act. To pursue something I believed I was meant to do. And for a while that's exactly what it was. A new city. New energy. New possibility. The feeling that the life I was supposed to be living was finally within reach.

Then gradually, quietly, in the way it happens when you love someone and want them to win, I started putting my own life on hold.

It happened slowly, the way the most costly things do. Just the accumulation of choosing their direction over mine. Helping someone find their purpose while mine waited. Working to hold everything together while my own dreams stayed on the shelf. Telling myself it was temporary. That my time was coming. That love required this kind of sacrifice and I was willing to make it.

Years passed, and it wasn't until right before everything fell apart that I started going to auditions again. Started pursuing what I had originally come there for. Started remembering I came to LA for something that had nothing to do with taking care of someone else's life.

Then it ended.

Not cleanly. The betrayal I discovered made the sacrifice feel even heavier in hindsight. Years of choosing someone else's direction. Years of deferring my own becoming. And the thing I had been sacrificing for turned out not to have been what I thought it was.

Then the pandemic hit and shut everything down and I found myself in a strange suspended space. The relationship gone. Everything locked down. The dream deferred. Trying to figure out what any of it was for.

That season forced me to learn something I couldn't have learned any other way. You cannot love someone else into wholeness at the cost of your own.

Nayyirah Waheed wrote something that stopped me when I first read it. You do not have to set yourself on fire to keep others warm.

That's not a metaphor when you've actually done it. When you've looked back at a season and seen clearly how much of yourself you quietly burned through trying to keep something else alive. How much of your direction, your dreams, your becoming you deferred because the person next to you needed more of you than you were keeping for yourself.

Not love failing. Self abandonment dressed up as love.

I came back to Houston, not as a defeat but as a return, to something real, to family, to the community that had been waiting, to the purpose that had never actually left, just been deferred while I was busy taking care of everything else.

But here's what nobody tells you about coming home to yourself after a long season away. It's disorienting.

The city had changed. My friendships had changed. And I had changed more than I realized. When you spend years inside a relationship that consumes a large part of who you are, your interests become your shared interests. Your world becomes your shared world. Your identity gets quietly tangled up with someone else's until you can't fully separate what was yours and what was just part of being with them.

Coming back to Houston meant I had to answer questions I hadn't asked in years.

What do I actually like, not what did we like. What are my interests.

That work is unglamorous. Nobody writes songs about the Tuesday afternoon when you sit alone and try to remember what music you actually loved before someone else's taste became the soundtrack of your life. Nobody makes movies about the slow process of reestablishing friendships that had gone quiet during years when someone else's needs took priority.

For me it looked like frozen yogurt. Specifically the Pinkberry in River Oaks. Frozen yogurt was something I did a lot back in LA with Maliyah, we'd go get yogurt together and I got completely hooked on the pomegranate flavor topped with fruit popping boba, granola, nuts, and a couple gummy bears. That was my shit. Something about that specific combination just hit different every single time. When I came back to Houston and everything with my heart happened and the LVAD and all of it I wasn't doing any of that anymore. I wasn't doing much of anything that was just for me. It wasn't until maybe six months to a year post op that I even thought about it again. Found out the River Oaks spot was open and just started going. Solo. A cup of my usual and a chair on the patio and nobody else's agenda competing for my attention. I'd sit there and people watch and let my thoughts slow down and just be still for a minute. No pressure to perform. No one to take care of. Just me, the yogurt, whatever was actually on my mind when I gave it space to show up, and whatever was happening on that stretch of River Oaks on a Tuesday afternoon. It sounds small. It was everything. That's what choosing yourself looks like in the ordinary moments. Not a grand gesture. A Tuesday afternoon, a cup of pomegranate froyo with popping boba, and the quiet decision to give yourself the same presence you've been giving everyone else. That's where I learned how to date myself. How to grab a burger alone or sit at a restaurant solo without it feeling like something was wrong. The Pinkberry closed down eventually, one of many froyo spots that shut down nationwide, and I won't even pretend I wasn't a little sad about that. Some places hold more than just the food. I'ma open my own yogurt shop one day. Just watch. Even though I'll probably go bankrupt getting high on my own supply. That joint gonna be jumping though. Pomegranate and popping boba from day one baby.

Nobody prepares you for that quiet reconstruction. Shit, nobody tells you how disorienting it is to have to figure all this shit out, like who the hell you actually are again, when you're not being partly defined by someone else anymore. What you find in that space, if you're willing to sit in it instead of running from it, is usually more purely yourself than anything that existed before.

The loss produces the clarity.

That's what coming back to Houston gave me too. In the daily practice of rediscovering myself something started to clarify. What I actually cared about. What I actually wanted. Who I actually was when I wasn't performing strength for someone else or building someone else's dream.

That return was the beginning of choosing myself, not perfectly, not without grief for what the season had cost, but honestly, with the understanding that what was happening through the pain of that ending was positioning me for something that required me to be more fully myself than I had been in years.

James Baldwin had a way of saying the unpolished truth in a way nobody else could. He wrote that it took many years of vomiting up all the filth I'd been taught about myself before I was able to walk on the earth as though I had a right to be here.

Choosing yourself isn't just about what you give to others. It's about stopping the running. Stopping the performance of being okay with what's quietly costing you everything. At some point you have to stop running from what you actually need and decide to give it to yourself.

The version of you that gives, loves, and shows up most completely is not the depleted version running on empty for everyone else. It's the whole version. The one that has been taken care of. The one that has chosen itself enough to have something real to offer.

Self betrayal is quiet. It's when you know what you need and override it anyway. When you know a situation isn't right and you stay because leaving feels harder than hurting. Every time you do it something erodes. The trust you have in yourself. The self respect that is the foundation of everything else healthy in your life.

Small betrayals become patterns. Patterns become identity. And one day you look at yourself and realize you've spent so long putting yourself last that you don't fully know what first feels like anymore.

Getting back there requires a decision, not a grand gesture or a dramatic announcement, just a quiet honest commitment that you matter, that your life deserves your own investment, that the dream you put on hold is still worth pursuing even now. Especially now.

That work doesn't belong to me alone. Everybody has a version of a life they quietly put on hold.

Where have you put yourself on hold? Where you've been so focused on managing everything around you that you stopped showing up for yourself the way you show up for everyone else.

What interests did you trade for shared ones? Which friendships went quiet while you were busy investing in someone else's world? What version of yourself is still waiting for you to come back?

You don't have to have it all figured out to start. You just have to make one choice. Today. One choice that says I matter enough to do this differently.

The life you want to live, the love you want to give, the person you're still becoming, all of it requires you to be whole. You cannot be whole while you're constantly leaving yourself behind.

Choose yourself, not instead of the people you love, but so you don't lose yourself trying to love them.

You are still going. Don't leave yourself behind this time. Coming back to yourself doesn't mean everything snaps back into place. Some of what you were before is gone. And learning to let that be okay is its own kind of work.

Chapter 12 — Growth Feels Like Loss at First

What happens to a dream deferred? Does it dry up like a raisin in the sun?

— Langston Hughes

Nobody warns you about this part.

They tell you growth is good. That change is necessary. That becoming a better version of yourself is worth pursuing. All of that is true.

But what they leave out, the part that catches most people completely off guard, is that growth often feels terrible before it feels like anything resembling freedom.

It feels like loss, like something being taken rather than something being gained, like the life you knew, even the parts that weren't serving you, disappearing before the new thing has fully arrived to replace it.

In that in between space, after the old thing has gone and before the new thing has taken shape, most people panic. They interpret the discomfort as a sign that something has gone wrong. That they should go back to what was familiar even if what was familiar was slowly diminishing them.

They don't recognize the discomfort for what it actually is. Evidence that something real is changing.

I've had to grieve the version of me I thought I'd be by now.

The man with the perfect health. The wife. A rhythm of life that made sense. The timeline I had mapped out in my head since I was young enough to have a vision for my future.

That version didn't happen. And letting it go was painful in a way that surprised me because it wasn't grief for something I had lost. It was grief for something that never came.

That's a specific kind of loss that doesn't get talked about enough. The mourning of the future you planned. A version of yourself you were certain you were building toward. The life that looked inevitable from the starting line and then quietly, gradually, stopped being the direction things were going.

Grieving that doesn't mean you've given up. It means you're being honest about the distance between what you hoped for and what is actually real. And that honesty is the first honest step toward building something that actually fits who you are now rather than who you thought you'd be.

The plan didn't survive. But the purpose did. But here's what makes my grief sit differently than most.

I think about my brothers. Nick was an author in his heart. He devoured books. He had the mind for it, the imagination, the storytelling instinct. He wanted to write the way Stephen King and Clive Barker write. Dark, layered, worlds built from the inside out. That was in him. I knew it. He knew it.

Life took him down a different path. The responsibilities. Different seasons. The way time moves faster than plans and before you know it the dream that was supposed to be temporary has been on hold for so long it starts to feel permanent. And then one day it just gets buried. Not dramatically. Quietly. The way most dreams die, under the weight of everything else that needed attention first. Langston Hughes asked what happens to a dream deferred. Nick and Jule are the answer I live with.

Jule was a gifted rapper. An artist with something real to say and a voice to say it with. I've heard him. I know what he had. That gift was genuine and specific and it was his in a way that nobody else could replicate. His life took him somewhere else too.

Both of my brothers went to their graves with buried gifts. The talent was real. The dreams were real. Life just has a way of filling up the space between wanting something and doing it until the wanting gets quiet and then quieter and then one day it just stops speaking.

I think about that in the middle of the night. More than I've ever said out loud until now. I think about Nick not writing his books, Jule not recording his music, two men who had real gifts, real dreams, real things to offer the world, who for whatever combination of reasons and seasons and life happening the way it happens, didn't get to live those things out. And I think about myself sitting here with this LVAD running, writing this book.

I don't have the luxury of burying my gifts. Not because I'm better than my brothers. Because I watched what happens when you do and I refuse to let that be my story too. Every word of this book is partly for them. Every time I show up and build and create and refuse to let the LVAD and the waiting and the uncertainty become an excuse to go quiet, I'm doing it for me and I'm doing it for them.

I'm living out loud for three. Not pressure. Purpose.

I've been rerouted, and most days I believe there's purpose in the path I'm actually on even when I can't see where it's going yet.

Growth requires you to outgrow things, and that sounds obvious until you're actually living it, until the thing you're outgrowing is a version of yourself that felt safe, a belief that gave you comfort even if it was keeping you small, a timeline you were clinging to even after life had made it clear the timeline wasn't yours to control.

Outgrowing things is the natural and necessary result of becoming. But it can feel like betrayal in the moment. Because what you're losing is real even when what you're gaining is better.

Losing that, even when losing it is the right thing, deserves to be grieved honestly. You are allowed to grieve what you're outgrowing while still choosing to grow.

There are moments I feel behind, like I'm playing catch up while everyone else is running ahead, building families, hitting milestones, moving through the stages of life in the order they were supposed to go.

That measuring never leads anywhere worth going.

The person you're measuring yourself against has a whole story underneath the highlight you're seeing. Private sacrifices. Quiet struggles. Detours that never made it onto the timeline you're comparing yours to. The milestones they hit on schedule may not be the milestones that were meant for your specific life.

Your path is not behind someone else's. It's just yours. Yours has been building something in you that the straight road never could have produced.

I've questioned God's timing more than once.

Asked why things haven't shifted yet. Why I'm still waiting. Why the version of life I've been working toward keeps arriving in pieces instead of all at once.

But even through the doubt I've never been left empty.

That's the gift of long suffering. The capacity to endure over time without bitterness. To keep belief alive in something you can't fully see yet. To move forward on faith when evidence is thin and the timeline makes no sense.

The waiting is doing something to you that the quick arrival never could. It's building the kind of character that can actually hold what's coming.

Not everyone who starts the journey with you is meant to finish it with you.

Some people are chapter people not whole book people. And recognizing that, grieving it honestly, and continuing to grow anyway is one of the hardest and most necessary things you will do.

Some relationships can't hold the new you. Some environments that once felt like home start to feel like a ceiling. That's not a sign something is wrong.

Not a sign that something is wrong. A sign that something is right.

Think about where you are right now. The thing that feels like it's falling apart. The timeline that didn't survive. A version of yourself that didn't arrive on schedule. The dream that has been quiet longer than you intended.

What if something is actually going right? What if what feels like falling apart is actually falling into place?

What gift have you been letting go quiet? Because life kept filling up the space where it was supposed to live and somewhere along the way the wanting got buried under everything else.

It's not too late to unbury it.

Growth doesn't announce itself as growth. At first it announces itself as disruption. As the grief of the version of yourself that didn't happen. As the loss of what was familiar.

And then one day after enough honest forward motion you look back and understand what was actually happening while you were just trying to survive it.

You were becoming. What felt like loss wasn't loss. It was clearance. Knowing that doesn't make the hard mornings easier. It just changes what you do with them. Langston Hughes asked what happens to a dream deferred and I used to read that as a cautionary question. Now I read it as a personal one. Nick's books never got written. Jule's music never got recorded. I sit with that every time I open a document and start a sentence. The dream doesn't die, it just goes quiet and waits to see if you're ever coming back for it. That's the real question underneath the poem. Not what happens to the dream. What happens to you while you're waiting to go get it.

Chapter 13 — Remove the Choice

I can do all things through Christ who strengthens me.

— Philippians 4:13

There are days when the weight is present before you open your eyes.

Just there. The quiet reality of something unresolved pressing in before the day has even started. And life doesn't pause for it. People still need you. The day still calls for something.

The world keeps moving whether the feeling shows up or not.

That's when you find out what you're actually made of, not in the moments that feel good, but in the ones that don't.

And if you're honest, you've been there too. That space where you don't feel like you have anything left to give but life is still asking something from you anyway.

I'm human. I feel things and I feel them deeply. There are mornings where the weight is there before I even sit up. Where the reality of everything unresolved, the health situation, the finances, the uncertainty, presses in all at once and the simplest things require a conscious decision.

I get up anyway, not because I've figured out how to stop feeling it, but because I know what's at stake, because I've been gifted something most people take for granted without realizing they're doing it. The gift of life.

I can't justify not getting up, not building, not showing up for what I've been given just because the feeling wasn't there on a particular morning.

I know what removing the choice looks like at its most extreme because I live this shit. When they accepted me for the LVAD they said recovery typically runs four to six weeks, sometimes closer to two months. I just smiled to myself, hold my beer I thought.

I asked what the fastest anyone had ever been discharged after LVAD surgery was.

They said fourteen days.

I didn't even blink. Fuck nah. I said it with a smirk. "Gimme thirteen and I'll be home."

They probably didn't take me seriously. That's okay. Thirteen days later I walked out. That's not a medical statistic. That's what happens when the choice gets made before the circumstances show up to negotiate with you.

And I learned what that actually looks like in practice not from some big dramatic moment but from a Sunday morning that almost didn't happen. A few weeks after Hannah first brought me to church I was going back on my own. Third or fourth Sunday. I woke up, got dressed, headed out. Then I found out Hannah wasn't going to make it that day.

I sat with that for a minute. That shy kid feeling came back. The one I thought I'd long outgrown. Not shyness exactly. More like the thing I've done my whole life, pulling back, dimming down, making room for whoever else is in the space. I command every room I walk into and I've known that since I was young, but I've spent just as long instinctively pulling back from it out of consideration for whoever else is there working hard for what comes to me naturally. I've been doing it so long it happens before I decide to. Standing outside that church alone it happened again. The quiet embarrassment of not wanting to walk into a room full of people alone. Not wanting to figure out where to sit or who to talk to or how to navigate a space that still felt new without someone I knew beside me.

I almost turned around. But I went anyway.

I walked into that church alone, nervous in a way I hadn't expected to feel, and something happened that I didn't anticipate. The church was large. The kind of place where you can feel small just walking through the doors. But the moment I stepped inside people welcomed me. Not in a performance way. Genuinely. Like I belonged there before I had done anything to earn belonging.

I found a seat. The family to my right and the man to my left naturally pulled me into the service. Somewhere in the middle of it I found myself holding hands with strangers in worship and prayer and I didn't feel strange about it. I felt settled.

Then came the moment in the service where they invite anyone who wants to become a member to come forward.

The man beside me leaned over and mentioned he had joined a couple weeks before. Encouraged me to do the same. The woman on my right and her family joined in gently. All of them nudging me toward something I had actually been thinking about for a few weeks already.

I hesitated. If you know me you know I don't go looking for attention. I attract it naturally but I don't seek it. And walking forward in that church meant going down the center aisle with everyone watching, your face on the giant screen at the front. That wasn't something I was ready for.

The woman beside me saw it without me saying a word.

She leaned in quietly and told me I didn't have to walk down the middle. There were ushers at the side. I could walk out the side door instead and still join.

She gave me a way through that fit exactly who I am. I took it. I walked to the side. I joined the church.

I've been a member since. When I can't make it in person I watch the sermons on YouTube. Pastor Keon has become someone whose voice I carry with me. None of it would have happened if I had turned around that morning when I found out Hannah wasn't coming.

Removing the choice looks like that in real life. Just deciding before the feeling shows up that you're going to go anyway. That the discomfort of showing up alone is smaller than the cost of not showing up at all.

There's a difference between inspiration and intention that nobody talks about enough.

Inspiration is a feeling. It comes and goes on its own schedule and it does not check in with you before it leaves. You can't manufacture it. You can't force it to show up when you need it most. If you're waiting on it to move you will be waiting a long time.

Intention is a decision. It doesn't require a feeling to back it up. It just requires you to have already decided.

Have you decided yet? That's the whole question, not whether you feel ready, not whether the circumstances are favorable, not whether the weight has lifted or the outcome has shown up or the feeling has returned. Have you decided.

There are days when it doesn't feel inspirational. Days when it just feels heavy. The heaviness is real. The moments where it's just you and your thoughts and the quiet and you can feel the health situation and the finances and the uncertainty pressing in, those are real.

Sitting in that space and feeling the full weight of what it means to keep going when going is hard, that's not weakness.

That's the cost of being someone who gives a damn. Heavy taught me something though.

Empty means you've poured everything out. Given and shown up and fought and carried more than most people will ever know. Empty is what happens to people who actually give a damn.

If you're still here, still breathing, still getting up even when you don't feel like it, you're not done. You're in a different kind of season. A season where you don't move because it feels right. You move because it's already been decided.

I remove the choice.

On the days when the feeling isn't there, when inspiration has left the building and the weight is heavy and the outcome is still uncertain, I don't negotiate with myself about whether to get up. The choice was already made. I'm grateful for the day I was given so

I'm going to go live it. Regardless of what the day calls for. Regardless of how it feels.

My mother has already buried two sons. My brother Mike has already lost enough. The people in the middle of their own fight right now who are watching how I carry mine and deciding what's possible for theirs, those are my faces. That's not inspiration. That's a covenant. Philippians 4:13 says I can do all things through Christ who strengthens me. On the mornings when I have nothing left that's not motivation. That's the only math that makes the numbers work.

Now think about yours.

Who are the faces that get you up on the days when getting up costs something? Who is the person in your life that needs you here more than they need anything else you could ever offer them?

Who is the younger version of you still waiting to see if you're going to come through?

Find those faces. Write them down if you have to. Put them somewhere you'll see them on the mornings when the feeling isn't there and the weight is present and every part of you wants to stay still.

That's your covenant. It's more powerful than any feeling motivation could ever produce.

You are not done. You just feel empty, and empty means you've been giving, empty means you've been fighting, empty means you are exactly the kind of person who shows up even when showing up costs everything.

The strength you're looking for isn't going to arrive before you move. It's going to arrive because you moved.

You don't wait for it to come back and then get up. You get up and it comes back.

So remove the choice. Move for them. Move for yourself. Not because it feels good. Because it's already decided.

You have little to give and everything to gain. That's where something unbreakable gets built. And once something unbreakable is built in you, it doesn't stay yours. It starts to radiate.

Chapter 14 — Become the Light You Needed

The marathon continues.

— Nipsey Hussle

Someone needed you once and you showed up.

Maybe you didn't feel ready. Maybe you were in the middle of your own hard thing. But you showed up anyway and something you said or did or simply the way you carried yourself gave someone else something they needed to keep going. You may not have even known you did it.

It doesn't announce itself or require a stage or a perfectly constructed story with a clean ending. It just radiates from whoever is willing to carry it

I'm writing this chapter from inside the dark.

Not metaphorically. Literally. As these words are being written I'm inactive on a heart transplant list because of insurance and financial circumstances still being worked through. The LVAD is still running. The uncertainty is present. Real weight sitting on all of it. The situation has not resolved.

And I'm writing anyway.

I didn't wait to be healed to be helpful. People expect you to be broken by something like this.

They expect fear, weakness, someone visibly diminished by what they're carrying. And when you're not, when you show up with energy and purpose and a genuine smile and a life that looks like it's moving forward instead of falling apart, people don't always know what to do with that.

I get messages regularly from people who are genuinely confused by how I move. How are you so positive. How are you so carefree. How do you live like everything is okay.

And my answer is always the same. Because everything is okay. Everything is exactly how it's supposed to be.

Not because the circumstances are easy. They're not. There is weight. But because I've made peace with where I am and I trust where I'm going and I refuse to let what's uncertain steal the life that's already here.

People watch that and something happens in them.

Some of them have watched a brother or a father go through the same things I'm living with. They send me messages telling me they wish their person had lived to meet me. That they wish they could have seen what I carry and how I carry it. That maybe it would have changed something. Maybe it would have given them a different lens to look through.

I carry those messages with weight, because it isn't just someone saying something kind. It's someone telling me that my life, the way I live it, has become a mirror for what's possible. That a man on a transplant waiting list with an LVAD humming in his chest can still be a source of light for the people around him. That surviving doesn't have to look like suffering.

Other people find my platform while searching for information to help a sick loved one. They're in research mode, looking for anything that might help the person they love understand what they're facing. And somehow they land on me. And they send my pages to their family member. For hope. For proof that the thing their loved one is carrying doesn't have to define them. That someone else is living it and still building and still smiling and still here.

That's your story becoming someone else's lifeline. Not after you figured it out. While you're still figuring it out.

And then there are the hospital visits.

I have been a patient more times than I care to count. Rooms I didn't choose, circumstances I didn't plan for, stays that interrupted everything and forced me to be still when being still is the last thing I wanted. And somewhere in those visits something consistent happened.

I became the favorite patient.

Not because I was the easiest or the least complicated medically. Because of how I showed up in those rooms. The nurses would tell the other patients about me. Come meet this guy. Come talk to him. He's going through something and you'd never know it. He'll give you something to hold onto.

I walk back in for another visit and other patients recognize me. Not from the news or a viral moment or anything I planned. Just from being there before. From having been a presence that left something behind. They remember me. They call out to me. Some of them light up. A man with an LVAD running, waiting on a heart, walking into a hospital and being recognized by the people who are also waiting, also fighting, also trying to hold on.

Nothing about it was engineered. It just happens when you carry your circumstances with grace instead of letting them carry you. When you decide that the room you're in, whatever room it is, deserves the best version of you even on the days when showing up costs everything.

I've also watched something happen over the last few years that I didn't anticipate but that I believe with everything in me is connected to what I've been doing.

Since I started being transparent about my journey more and more people have started doing the same. People sharing their health battles. Their life obstacles. The things they were hiding because they were afraid of what transparency would cost them. And now they're letting it out. Living in their stories instead of behind them.

I know I'm a catalyst for that, not because I'm special, but because I went first, because I chose to live out loud in a season where going quiet would have been the easier and more understandable choice. And when people see someone carry something hard without being destroyed by it, without hiding it, without letting it become the whole story, something shifts in them about what's possible for their own life.

The ripple. What it means to become the light. You don't have to save anyone. You don't have to have the answers. You just have to be willing to let your real life be visible to people who need proof that a real life can hold this much weight and still be worth living.

Think about your darkest moment.

Not the hardest physically. The darkest internally. The moment where the weight was heaviest and the uncertainty was loudest and you were looking for something to hold onto.

What did you need in that moment? Not a solution, not someone with all the answers, something simpler and more essential than that.

You needed to know you weren't alone in it. You needed someone whose existence was proof that the darkness wasn't permanent. Someone who had been somewhere like where you were and survived it. Someone who could look you in the eye and say I know what this feels like and I promise you it doesn't stay this dark forever.

That's the light you needed, and someone out there right now, in the middle of something that feels exactly like what you've already been through, needs that same light from you.

People don't need answers. They need evidence. Your survival is the evidence.

Nipsey Hussle understood something about service that I carry with me. He didn't wait until he had everything figured out to start building for his community. He worked from inside the struggle. Served from exactly where he was with exactly what he had. Invested in the people around him while his own path was still uncertain.

The marathon continues, not after you cross the finish line, but during the race, while your legs are tired and the end isn't visible yet and the only thing keeping you moving is the conviction that what you're building matters.

That's the philosophy I'm living right now. Running the marathon while the outcome is still uncertain. Writing this book not because

I've arrived somewhere but because the running itself is the service.

Becoming the light doesn't require what most people think it requires, not fame, not a platform, not a published book or a stage or a perfectly constructed story with a clean ending, not having all your wounds healed before you show them. Just willingness.

Willingness to be honest about where you've been. To show up for someone in their darkness the way you needed someone to show up in yours. To let your survival mean something beyond your own relief.

A conversation. A phone call. A message to someone who is in the middle of something you've already been through. A willingness to say me too when someone is ashamed of something you've carried yourself.

That's light, simple, human, irreplaceable light, and the world is desperately short of it.

You have something to offer because of what you've been through, not after it, because of it.

The depth you carry. The wisdom you've earned the hard way. A specific quality of presence that only comes from having actually been somewhere real. The ability to sit with someone in their pain without flinching because you've already sat in your own.

That's not something you can manufacture or buy or fast track. It only comes one way. Through the fire.

Which means everything you've been through, every dark night, every season that tested you, every moment you wanted to quit and didn't, has been preparing you for something beyond your own survival. It has been preparing you to be someone else's light.

The LVAD is still running. The transplant hasn't come. The financial situation is still being worked through and the uncertainty is still very much present. I'm not waiting until it's fixed or until I'm on the other side of it looking back with the luxury of distance. I'm doing it now, from the middle of it, with everything still unresolved and everything still uncertain and everything still requiring more faith than certainty.

This book is my survival turned into service. My darkness turned toward your light.

My still going through it offered freely to the person who needs to know it's possible to keep going.

You don't have to wait for the morning to be someone's light. You just have to keep going.

In the keeping going, in the refusing to quit, in the choosing to build something meaningful from inside a season that gave you every reason not to, you become exactly what someone else needs.

The light you needed, given freely, from inside the dark.

For every dark night there is a bright day. Keep going. The morning is coming.

Fueled by Love.

Cliff

Fueled by Love

Photo by Gerrick Walker | @gerrickwalkerimages

A Letter To You

Weeping may endure for a night, but joy comes in the morning.

— Psalm 30:5

I don't know your name.

I don't know exactly what brought you to this book or what you were carrying when you picked it up or what season of your life you're in right now. I don't know if you're reading this from a place of quiet struggle or loud crisis or somewhere in between where everything looks fine on the outside but feels uncertain on the inside.

But I know you picked this up for a reason. And I believe that reason matters more than you know.

I want to talk to you for a moment not as an author and not as someone who has figured everything out but as a human being who has been in the dark and found something worth holding onto and wants more than anything to make sure you find it too.

First I want to speak to the person living in fear.

The quiet kind of fear. The kind that lives underneath the surface of a life that looks okay from the outside. Fear of the unknown. The fear that comes with uncertainty, with not knowing how things are going to unfold, with carrying something unresolved for so long that the not knowing has become its own kind of weight.

I understand that fear from the inside. I have lived with uncertainty about my own future for years. Living with the LVAD and not knowing exactly how the story ends. Fear of the unknown is not a concept to me. It is a daily companion that I have had to learn to carry without letting it drive.

Fear of the unknown grows in the absence of purpose. When you have something real to move toward, something that matters and requires your presence, the fear doesn't disappear but it loses its authority over your decisions. You stop organizing your life around what might go wrong and start organizing it around what you're building. Fear doesn't leave. It just gets smaller relative to the thing you're building.

The antidote to fear of the unknown is not certainty. You may never have certainty. The antidote is meaning. A reason to keep moving that is bigger than the fear trying to hold you still.

You are not behind. The timeline we had in our heads, the version of life we planned that didn't materialize, the feeling that everyone else is where they're supposed to be and you somehow missed a turn, that feeling is lying to you. You are exactly where your specific journey has brought you, with all its detours and disruptions and seasons that didn't go the way you planned, shaping something in you that the straight path never could have produced. Trust that.

Trust that.

I also want to say something to the person who is exhausted.

Not physically tired. Soul tired. The kind of exhaustion that comes from carrying something heavy for a long time without enough rest and without enough people who truly understand what you're carrying. The kind where you're still showing up every day, still functioning, still taking care of everything and everyone that needs you, but privately you are running on something close to empty and you don't know how much longer you can keep going at this pace.

Needing rest is not weakness. Needing support is not failure. And needing somebody to just sit with you in it for once, that's not asking too much either.

You are allowed to need things, to say I'm not okay right now without immediately following it with but I'll be fine, to let people love you the way you love them. You are allowed to receive.

There is a scene in the movie Troy where a messenger boy tells Achilles he wouldn't want to fight the giant warrior they're up against. Achilles looks at him and says that's why no one will remember your name. I'm not Achilles. But I am a warrior. And I understand now what he meant. The story you're willing to live, the one that costs you something real, is the only story worth telling. They made that movie to tell the story of a man from 400 BC and people are watching it to this day. Feeling it. Learning from it. That's what a real story does. It outlives the person who lived it. This book is my story. Not the finished version because that version doesn't exist yet. But the version being lived right now, in real time, with an LVAD humming and a transplant on the way and everything uncertain and everything worth showing up for. I don't need to be remembered as the man who beat the odds. I just need this book to find the person who needs it long after I'm gone and hand them something worth holding onto. That's how you live forever. Not in monuments. In the moments you gave someone else the courage to keep going.

I also want to say something to the person who has been waiting for permission to start.

To write the thing they've been sitting on. To finally say what they've been waiting to say. To start before the fear gets smaller or the timing gets better, because it won't.

The world is ready. You are ready, not because you have it all figured out, but because you have something real to offer and the people who need it are waiting even though they don't know your name yet.

Start now, not Monday, not when things settle down or when you feel more prepared, but right now from exactly where you are with exactly what you have, because the version of you that keeps waiting is costing the world something it needs.

And finally I want to say something to everyone.

Whatever you're going through right now, however dark the night feels, however long the storm has been going, however tired you are of holding on without being able to see what you're holding on for.

Hold on.

Not because I can promise you how it ends. Not because I have a guarantee that everything works out the way you're hoping. But because I know from the inside of a life that has given me every reason to let go that there is always something on the other side of the darkness worth being present for.

Always.

You don't have to have it figured out before you move. You don't have to be healed before you help somebody. You can do all of it from right inside the middle of it, because that's where the most honest version of your story lives, not on the other side looking back, but right here in the middle of still going through it.

The morning is not a metaphor. It is a daily reality. It comes without fail. Without exception. Regardless of how long or how complete the night was.

You need to be here when it arrives. So stay. Keep going. Let love fuel you when nothing else can.

Trust that the story you're living, messy and unfinished and not yet what you hoped it would be, is still being written.

I'm rooting for you. Genuinely. From one person who is still in it, still living with the fear, still choosing to build anyway, to another.

If this book gave you something to hold onto and you want somewhere to take it, I built that too. The Chaos Code and the Built in Chaos Journal are waiting for you on the next page. They pick up right where this ends.

Fueled by Love.

Cliff

Author's Note

The LVAD is a Left Ventricular Assist Device. In plain terms it's a mechanical pump living inside my chest doing the work my heart can't do on its own. Turns out I was sicker than I even knew. My heart was struggling to pump blood the way it's supposed to and was on the verge of completely failing so they installed this thing in me while we wait for a new heart.

It's not a replacement. Think of it more like a very expensive, very serious babysitter that was never supposed to stay this long. My cardiologist would probably describe it differently but I like my version better. Lowkey this is my superhero origin story. I'm basically Iron Man.

The specific device is called the Medtronic HVAD. Implanted March 10, 2021. Eighty-five days after that surgery I got a call and a letter from my hospital informing me that Medtronic had discontinued the device and pulled it from the market entirely. The reason? Reports of higher rates of neurological complications including strokes compared to other available devices, along with concerns about the complexity of the implant procedure itself. They ceased all distribution and notified physicians to stop new implants immediately. Straight BULLSHIT. The thing keeping my heart going was no longer being manufactured. That was a lot to sit with. And the wild part is five years later my heart still hasn't recovered enough for it to be removed without a transplant being available. Still in my chest. Still running. I made peace with that. God's got me.

Being on the transplant waitlist isn't what most people picture. I'm currently listed as a Status 4 which generally means stable and supported by a device. Then there's the blood type situation. I'm O positive which means I can donate to almost anybody but not everybody can donate to me. The pool is smaller than you'd think and the wait is real.

Here's the part I want you to understand without feeling sorry for me. As of this writing I'm listed but inactive. Insurance. A heart transplant costs close to two million dollars and the system requires coverage before you can receive one. I'm not telling you this for sympathy. I'm telling you because this entire book is built on honesty and leaving this part out would be a contradiction. I'm actively working through it and I will get back to active status. Note: You may notice that earlier in this book, particularly in the Prologue, I reference being on the transplant list. That was accurate at the time those words were written. This book was written in real time across multiple seasons and my status changed during that process. The inactive status referenced here reflects where things stand as of publication. The story is live. So is the fight.

I wrote this because I want to help people. Since this season of my life went public I've heard from hundreds who told me something I shared helped them or someone they love get through something hard. I want to reach more of those people. They say how many people you bless is how you measure success. If this book reaches one and teaches one and helps one then it did exactly what it was supposed to do.

And if I'm being completely honest, what if telling my story doesn't just help others but also saves me? If this book does what it's meant to do, imagine that.

Fueled by Love.
Cliff

About the Author

Cliff "The Gift" Wallace is a Houston-based author, actor, content creator, fitness professional, public speaker, and founder of the Fueled by Love Foundation. Known for his authenticity and relentless positivity, Cliff has built a community of hundreds of thousands across social media by showing up honestly through one of life's greatest tests. Currently living with an LVAD while awaiting a heart transplant, he doesn't write from the other side of hardship. He writes from inside it, in real time, for everyone still in the middle of their own storm. Fueled by Love is his first book.

Instagram: @iamcliffthegift

TikTok: @iamcliffthegift

Facebook: @iamcliffthegift

About This Book

What if the thing standing between you and the life you want isn't your circumstances? What if it's the lens you're looking through?

Fueled by Love is not a book written from the comfort of the other side. It was written from inside the storm, by a man living with an LVAD keeping his heart beating, waiting on a transplant that hasn't come, building anyway, refusing to quit anyway, choosing love as fuel when everything else runs dry.

In these pages Cliff "The Gift" Wallace takes you through the perspective shifts, hard truths, and lived moments that have kept him moving through one of life's greatest tests. From accepting what is to choosing yourself, from silencing the voice that holds you back to becoming the light someone else needs, this book meets you exactly where you are and shows you what's possible from there. Not someday. Not from the other side. Right now. From inside it.

Fueled by Love.

Also by Cliff "The Gift" Wallace

The Chaos Code: Build Discipline Inside the Storm

Five pillars. Zero excuses. Built for the moments when life is falling apart and you need something you can actually use right now. Available on Kindle.

Built in Chaos: The Journal

Discipline When Life Is Falling Apart. A 90-day guided journal built around the five pillars of the Chaos Code. The companion system for putting it into daily practice. Available on Amazon.

What's Next

The principles I've built my life around during this season I call the Chaos Code. Five pillars. Show Up Anyway. Control What You Can. Stack Small Wins. Eliminate Excuses. Protect Your Mind. If this book moved you and you want to go deeper with the framework I broke the whole thing down in The Chaos Code: Built in Chaos, available on Kindle. It's a short read, straight to the point, built for the moments when life is falling apart and you need something you can actually use right now. If you're ready to put it into daily practice the Built in Chaos Journal: Discipline When Life Is Falling Apart is the 90 day companion system with prompts, trackers, and weekly check-ins built around all five pillars. Both pick up right where this book leaves off. Everything is available on Amazon. Links and more at cliffthegift.com. Fueled by Love. 🩶

Stay Connected

If this book moved you, share it. Leave a review. Tell somebody. That's how real things travel.

Find Cliff across all platforms @iamcliffthegift

Facebook | Instagram | TikTok | YouTube

For bulk orders, speaking inquiries, and foundation information visit

cliffthegift.com

Fueled by Love. 🩶